The Irreducible Minimum
An examination of basic Christian doctrine

David C. Myers

Wipf and Stock Publishers
EUGENE, OREGON

Wipf and Stock Publishers
199 West 8th Avenue, Suite 3
Eugene, Oregon 97401

The Irreducible Minimum
An Examination of Basic Christian Doctrine
By Myers, David C.
Copyright©2002 Myers, David C.
ISBN: 1-57910-279-4
Publication date: July, 2002
Previously published by NPP, 2002.

I would like to dedicate this book to my best friend; Sally, my wife.

And to my friends;

Pastor Clay Kahler
Pastor Steve Whitten
Chaplain Robert Freiberg
Mr. Ron Donofero
Mr. Parry Kleinsasser
Dr. Mark Chadwell

And to my favorite professors;

Dr. Marvin Lubenow
Dr. George Hare

Table of Contents

Table of Contents vii

List of Illustrations ix

List of tables ix

Foreword 11

Chapter One – Bibliology 13

Chapter Two - Dispensationalism 27

Chapter Three – Theology Proper & Trintarianism 33

Chapter Four - Christology 53

Chapter Five - Pneumatology 57

Chapter Six - Angelology 67

Chapter Seven - Anthropology 77

Chapter Eight - Hamartiology 103

Chapter Nine - Soteriology 111

Chapter Ten – Ecclesiology 117

Chapter Eleven – Eschatology 123

Appendixes

   A. Paul, model of a missionary 145

   B1. Research on ecclesiastical governmental forms,
       doctrines, and practices.... 153

B2. The Church and the Crusades 173

C. Exegetical word study: Babylon… 189

D. Selected Bibliography 204

List of Illustrations

Figure

1. Map of Asia Minor in Paul's day 148

List of Tables

Table

1. The Dispensations 30
2. The *Shema* 42
3. Ryrie's Trinitarian model 50
4. Prayer/Solitude chart from the Gospels 65
5. Jensen's Teachings of the Colossian Heresies 74
6. The Crusades 175

Foreword

It was the fall of 1999 when I first heard the term "Irreducible Minimum." The noted Bible teacher, Dr. George Goolde introduced the concept this way... "The irreducible minimum is the basic minimum amount of information that you must master in order to have truly learned this subject.

In this work, Pastor David C. Myers has undertaken the daunting task of boiling Christian doctrine down to it's irreducible minimum.

I have read this book twice and can confidently say that he has done just that. Whether you are a Pastor, who wants to equip the body, or a seminary student who is looking to get a jump on your program, or a Sunday school teacher who wishes to introduce your class to the basics, this book is for you.

Designed as a survey of the basic Christian doctrines, this book is destined to develop in the reader a hunger for more.

I met David in that class with Dr. Goolde. Since that time he has become my partner in ministry, my fellow teacher and my best friend. You have my personal guarantee, after having read "The irreducible Minimum," you will be all the richer.

Pastor Clay A. Kahler

Bibliology
Chapter One

Bibliology Proper

> All scripture is inspired by God, and profitable for doctrine, for reproof, for correction, for instruction in righteousness.
>
> -2 Timothy 3:16

> But know this first of all, that no prophecy of scripture was ever made by an act of human will, but men moved by the Holy Spirit from God.
>
> -2 Peter 1:20-21

Geisler and Nix, in their book *A GENERAL INTRODUCTION TO THE BIBLE* define inspiration as follows:

> Inspiration is that mysterious process by which the divine causality worked through the human prophets without destroying their individual personalities and styles to produce divinely authoritative and inspired writings.[1]

The sad truth is that no copies of the original autographs exist today. There are two extremes to the question of inerrancy. The first states that only the original autographs are inspired, while the second posits that all translations and copies are inspired. Norm Geisler gives what this writer considers to be the definitive answer:

> "Only the autographs were actually inspired; good copies are accurate." In order to avoid the two extremes of either an unattainable original or a fallible one, it must be asserted that a good copy or translation of the autographs is for all practical purposes the inspired word of God.[2]

While this author believes the former view, that is, that only the original autographs are inspired, too much emphasis can be placed on this fact, which can detract from the truth that the Bible used today is highly accurate. We do not know why God allowed no original autographs to exist. The text offers an interesting possibility. Mankind loves to worship objects. Many people are over-infatuated with nature, and tend to worship the created rather than the creator. A good example of this principle is found in scripture in 2 Kings 18:4:

> [4]He removed the high places and broke down the *sacred* pillars and cut down the Asherah. He also broke in pieces the bronze serpent that Moses had made, for until those days the sons

---

[1] Geisler and Nix, *A General Introduction to the Bible*, 39
[2] Geisler and Nix, 44

of Israel burned incense to it; and it was called Nehushtan.

The Roman Catholic and Eastern Orthodox churches unfortunate emphasis on relics such as the shroud of Turin, pieces of the original cross, and the bones of the saints, are another example of this principle. During the various crusades, certain rulers spent more time relic hunting then fighting! Professor John Robinson says the following, in regards to the outcome of the fifth crusade:

> The only leader who felt successful was King Andrew of Hungary. With his passion for religious relics, he perhaps thought that taking sacred objects back to Hungary would appease his people for the taxes forced out of them to pay for the Crusade. Now he had treasures of incalculable value to lay before them. The local dealers in relics must have offered up their own private prayers of thanksgiving to God for sending them this royal pigeon, who had exhausted his funds to purchase their wares. He was convinced that he was going home with the head of St. Stephen, the head of St. Margaret, the right hand of St. Thomas, the right hand of St. Bartholomew, one of the jugs that had held the water Jesus turned into wine at the wedding at Cana, and a piece of the staff of Aaron.[3]

So it can perhaps be seen why God would not allow the original autographs to survive. If man was so enamored with moldy old bones, imagine what he would do with the very words of the Creator! Yet God has said in Matthew 5:18:

---

[3] Robinson, John J. *Dungeon, Fire and Sword*. 237

> For truly I say unto you, until heaven and earth shall pass away, not the smallest letter or stroke shall pass away from the law, until all is accomplished.

So it can be seen that God has intended for His word to be preserved throughout the ages. Since one of God's attributes is that He cannot lie, and since he has stated in scripture that His word would be preserved, it follows that the Bible, as it is known today, is accurate and authoritative.

Old Testament Consistency

That the Old Testament is accurate is well documented. First and foremost, there are several complete manuscripts. Most of these date from the ninth century or later, but they are all fairly consistent. We know that the rules for transcribing the texts are extremely scrupulous. The Dead Sea scrolls verify portions of almost every book of the Old Testament, some copies dating clear back to the fourth century! The fragments date almost a thousand years earlier than other existing manuscripts, yet agree almost exactly. The Dead Sea Scrolls are an important verification, and were discovered in the middle of this century.

New Testament Consistency

The New Testament manuscripts are numerous, but are of poorer quality than the Old Testament manuscripts. There are thousands of Greek manuscripts, in various stages of completeness, scattered throughout the world. It is beyond the scope of this project to explain in detail the manuscript families, or to rehash the debate over the importance of the critical or majority texts. The important detail that must be remembered by the Christian is that there are virtually no doctrinal differences in contention between the text types.

The New Testament books were written during the second half of the first century. They were written on papyrus, and decayed fairly rapidly. Papyrus is a paper-like product made out of reeds, and decays rapidly, except under abnormal conditions. Copies were made, and then copies of copies, and distributed throughout the churches. None of the early copies have survived, for the same reasons that the original autographs have not survived. Persecutions by the various Roman Emperors didn't help matters, either. But the large numbers of manuscripts available help ensure that the Bible is as accurate as possible. Once more, we must return to God's promise, given in Matthew, chapter five, verse eighteen.

So the Bible, as we know it, is a series of translations copied from copies of copies of the original autographs, and verified by various methods, such as textual comparison/criticism of the surviving manuscripts, by theologians and historians. While there are countless translations currently in use, the most popular are, in no particular order, the New American Standard, the New King James Version, The King James Version, and the New International Version.

Summary of the basic precepts of Bibliology

While only the original autographs were inspired, or "God-Breathed," none of these have survived to the present day. We make the presupposition that the word of God is truth, and God's word says that:

1. God is incapable of untruth.

2. God assures us that his word will survive.

   For further elucidation on the attributes of God, as well as supporting scripture, see chapter three. Therefore, while not actually inspired, the Bible today is accurate, and authoritative, and profitable for doctrine, for reproof, for correction, and for instruction in righteousness.

Epistemology

In the day-to-day search for truth, God has given the believer sources: The Bible, and Illumination by the Holy Spirit. We know that, while human authors physically wrote the words, the Bible is actually inspired by God. The technical term for this is Dual-Authorship. We know that the bible is the inspired word of God because it tells us that it is. The technical term for this principle is Internal evidence. It is true that this is circular reasoning, or "begging the question", but some presuppositions are called for, and are justified by the authority of the word of God.

In the case of the born again Christian, he or she must make the presupposition that the Bible is true, and everything else follows. 1 Timothy 3:16-17 says:

> All scripture is inspired by God and profitable for teaching, for reproof, for training in righteousness; that the man of God may be adequate, equipped for every good work.

Inspiration is defined as that quality, inherent in the autographs of scripture, which render them as much the word of God as if God had breathed them personally breathed them out of his mouth. In the scripture quoted above, the word in Greek that becomes the English "inspired' is *theopneustos*; meaning literally "God-breathed". This is the only time that this particular word is used in scripture, and it's meaning is crystal clear.

The second source of truth for Christians is Illumination. Illumination differs from revelation. It is very important to note the difference between these two terms. Revelation is defined as the supernatural impartation of truth, from God to man, of that which man could not otherwise know. It follows, then, that not every dream, idea, or vision is a direct revelation from God! The Holy Spirit will reveal scriptural truth, which will give the Christian a clearer understanding of the meaning of scripture. Paul tells us, in Galatians 1:11-12 that God directly revealed truth to him. Here is the quote:

> For I would have you know, brethren, that the Gospel which was preached by me is not according to man. For I neither received it from man, nor was I taught it, but I received it through a revelation of Jesus Christ.

This scripture proves that there was such a thing as direct revelation. But as there are no apostles today, and as those with the gift of Prophecy (if indeed that gift still exists within the church) are difficult (or impossible) to find, it follows therefore that God will not directly reveal anything in this day and age. It is not necessary for believers today, because God has provided something for us that the early church did not have the scriptures in a complete form. Yet we know that in addition to the scriptures, the Lord has provided a real, vibrant form of assistance. Again, we know this, because the Bible tells us that it is so. 1 Corinthians 2:9-10 teaches that:

> But as it is written: "Eye has not seen, nor ear heard, nor have entered into the heart of man the things which God has prepared for those who love him." But God has revealed them to us through his spirit. For the spirit searches all things, yes, the deep things of God.

And in Acts, chapter 8:30-31 we see the Holy Spirit acting through Philip to the Ethiopian eunuch.

> And when Philip had run up, he heard him reading Isaiah the prophet; and said, "Do you

understand what you are reading?" And he said, "Well how could I unless someone guides me?" And invited Philip to come up and sit with him.

So far it has been demonstrated that there are two sources of truth that God offers to his children for instruction. They are (1) the Bible and (2) illumination from the Spirit. Illumination gives a clearer understanding of God's word than would otherwise be possible. Furthermore, the authority of scripture has been established through the explanation of dual-authorship. The next principle to be discussed is Interpretation. Paul tells us in 2 Timothy 2:15:

> Be diligent to present yourself approved to God
> as a workman who does not need to be ashamed,
> handling accurately the word of truth.

This passage illustrates the principle of interpretation. Interpretation is defined as the process of discerning the intended meaning of God's word by cutting a straight line through it. The study of Biblical Interpretation is called hermeneutics.

Historically, there are, and have been, two methods of interpreting the scriptures. These are called the allegorical method, and the literal method. These methods will be discussed in greater detail in the sections on dispensationalism and eschatology. For the present, it suffices to say that the author holds to the latter method. This is because the allegorical method assumes that scripture is so difficult to understand that what is says and what it means are two different things. This is not to say that there are no allegories in the literal method. Jesus used parables extensively. It is recognized that figurative language is also used. However, God intended the Bible to be understood by all men, to be used as the rule and guide for everyday life. In order for this to be possible, man must be able to have an understanding of scripture. This means that a literal, grammatically correct, and historical hermeneutic must be applied in order for "everyman" to be able to understand the meaning of God's word. Dr. David L. Cooper explains this principle as follows:

> When plain sense of scripture makes common sense, seek no other sense; therefor, take every word at its primary, ordinary, usual literal meaning unless the facts of the immediate context, studied in the light of related passages and axiomatic and fundamental truths, clearly indicate otherwise.[4]

Additionally, if scripture comes to us from God, and carries such authority, it follows that it is inerrant. If the Bible is the inspired, revealed word of the Almighty God, then it cannot contain errors. Nor can it contradict itself. Of course, unless one has knowledge of the original languages, then mistakes could occur within the translation, but this is not the same as mistakes within God's word. A careful, thorough study of how the bible came to us through history is proves that the Bible used by most believers today is as close to the original as is humanly possible, leaving little room for errors.

Canonicity is the recognition by man of the rule God instituted in His Word. This principle is backed up in the 24th chapter of Luke, Verses 44-45:

> Then he said to them, "These are the words which I have spoken to you while I was still with you, that all things must be fulfilled which are written in the Law of Moses and the Prophets concerning me." And He opened their understanding, that they might comprehend the scriptures.

---

[4] Shinn, Garland. Course Notebook; *Practical Biblical Hermeneutics.* 7

Many students have problems in the area of Canonicity. Why these sixty-six books? Who decided that the Bible as we know it is complete? Especially when confronted with the Apocrypha. It is important to remember that Canonicity is the recognition of inspiration, not the conferral thereof. That is, it is the recognition by God's people that He has inspired the writings.

Many people envision councils of theologians, resplendent in immaculate white robes and flowing beards, as conferring together in order to accept or reject scripture. This is simply not the case. The process was much more convoluted, spread out over several hundred years. But while the process varied, their were always three elements that applied. They are as follows:

1. Apostolic Authority. The book had to either be written by an apostle, or carry the authority of one. Thus, the book 1 Peter, being written by the apostle, required no other recommendation. (Other than being proven authentic). But Luke and Acts were supported by both Paul and Peter.

2. The book had to have been written before the end of the first century.

3. The book could not contradict other scripture.

Once it had been shown that the book in question met requirements one through three, the only thing left was universal recognition by the people of God.

What is the best way to study the Bible? The best way is to learn the original languages. Without doing that, then the inductive method is by far the best way. Using the inductive method, a believer studies the scripture without any preconceptions. He or she must be careful to study scripture within its context. Tools, such as lexical aids and commentaries are used to assist the believer in understanding the culture and manners of the original recipients, and the following questions are asked. Who was it written to? What is being said? Where was it written from, and where was it intended to be read? When was it written? And finally, Why was it written. Studies are made of difficult words within the text ask the same questions. For an example of a completed word study that looks at all aspects of a difficult concept, see appendix C. This process is called exegesis, and should be the ultimate goal of every student of the Bible.

Terms and definitions

Inspiration. That quality, inherent in the autographs of scripture, which render them as much the word of God as if God had breathed them personally breathed them out of his mouth. In the scripture quoted above, the word in Greek that becomes the English "inspired' is θεόπνευστος; meaning literally "God- breathed". This is the only time that this particular word is used in scripture, and its meaning is crystal clear. The passage that best illustrates this term is 2 Timothy 3:16.

Revelation. The supernatural impartation of truth from God to man of that which man could not otherwise know. It is best illustrated in scripture by 1 Corinthians 2:9-10.

Inscripturation. The process of putting the revealed word of God into the vocabularies of the human authors. This principle is best observed in 1 Corinthians 2:12-13.

Authority. The right of Scripture to demand of man compliance to the inspired word of God. See James 1:22.

Interpretation. Discerning the meaning of God's word by cutting a straight line through it. The best scriptural illustration for this principle is 2 Timothy 2:15.

Hermeneutics. This is defined as the science (principles) and art (task) by which the meaning of the biblical text is determined. Interpretation of scripture follows the literal-Grammatical-Historical method.

Canonicity. The recognition by man of the rule God instituted in His word. The best example in scripture to illustrate this principle is Luke chapter 24, verses 44-45.

Animation. The living quality inherent in the word of God as in no other book. It is the life transforming ability that is within the scriptures. See Hebrews 4:12.

Translation. Contextualizing the word of God from one language and culture to another so that it retains its meaning. Again, see 2 Tim. 2:15.

Illumination. Assistance given by the Holy Spirit, which enlightens man so that he applies the spiritual truths of the word. See John 16:13 for best example of this important principle.

Preservation. The principle, illustrated by John 10:35b, which insures the transmission of God's revelation so it retains its ability to act as God's word.

Infallible. Literally, "not fallible or breakable"; it refers to the divine character of scripture that necessitates its truthfulness.

Verbal, plenary inspiration. The doctrine holding that the very words of the bible are divested with divine authority and not merely thoughts or ideas. This term is broad in scope, and carries the idea that the entire document, that is, the bible is absolutely true in its entirety.

Dual authorship. The term used to describe the fact that, while God inspired the scriptures, and they are, literally, "God-breathed", humans penned them, and carry the style and vocabulary of that author. God used humans to write his words in legible characters.

Inerrant. This term applies to the original autographs only. That is to say, the original autographs were totally without error.

Dispensationalism
Chapter Two

Dr. Charles Ryrie defines a dispensation as follows, "A dispensation is a distinguishable economy in the outworking of God's purpose."[5] He explains the purpose of Dispensationalism as follows:

> Dispensationalism, then, claims to be a help in supplying the answer to the need for biblical distinctions, in offering a satisfying philosophy of history, and in employing a consistently normal principle of interpretation. These are basic areas in proper understanding of the Bible. If dispensationalism has the answers, then it is the most helpful tool in consistent biblical

---

[5] Ryrie, Charles. *Dispensationalism.* 19

interpretation. If not, then it ought to be minimized or discarded.[6]

The easiest way to explain the concept is to remember some of the attributes of God. He is immutable. That is, He is unchangeable. The same yesterday, today, and tomorrow. He cannot change. If he can, or does, then, by definition, He is not God. But we know that the rules change. While God remains constant, the rules for stewardship change as His ultimate plan unfolds. Dispensationalism cannot be placed within a single category. It effects countless other doctrines. It is a method of interpretation.

While the doctrine of dispensationalism can be difficult to define, there are three distinctions which help narrow the field of study and allow a proper focus. They are as follows:

1. The principle of interpreting scripture according to a literal, grammatical, historic hermeneutic. As Kahler says in *Simple Theology: Theology for the rest of us*, "A grammatical, historical, literal hermeneutic will inevitably result in a dispensational viewpoint.[7]"

2. Always remembering that there is a distinction between the church and Israel. Promises made to Israel apply to that nation, and that nation alone. This principle will be discussed in some detail in chapter eleven.

3. God's ultimate purpose for mankind is to bring glory to Himself. This is an important distinction between those who adhere to Dispensational theology, and those who practice covenentalism. A covenant theologian believes that God's ultimate purpose is to spread the Gospel.

---

[6] Ryrie, Charles. 20
[7] Kahler, Clay A. *Simple Theology; Theology for the rest of us.* 187

Acknowledgement of these specific dispensations is not essential to either the understanding, or adherence to, the tenants of this doctrine. Again, dispensationalism is too broad in scope to pin down to a single area of theology. That being said, both Scofield and Ryrie recognize seven distinct dispensations. They are as follows:

1. The dispensation of Innocency. This refers to Adam's condition before the fall. This allowed him to have a face-to-face relationship with God. This period is set forth in scripture in Genesis 1:28-3:36.

2. The Dispensation of Conscience. This economy is found in Genesis 4:1-8:14. Ryrie describes this period as follows:

> During this stewardship man was responsible to respond to God through the promptings of his conscience, and part of a proper response was to bring an acceptable blood sacrifice as God had taught him to do in Genesis 3:21 and 4:4. We have a record of only a few responding, and Abel, Enoch, and Noah are especially cited as heroes of faith.[8]

3. The Dispensation of Civil Government. This dispensation followed the flood, and resulted in the building of the tower of Babel, and the dispersion of the peoples of the earth by God. It was during this period that God selected Abraham to covenant with. The biblical description of this period is described in genesis 8:15-11:9.

4. The Dispensation of Promise, or Patriarchal Rule. This marks the beginning of God's dealings with His people Israel. See genesis 11:10-Exodus 18:27 for the narrative describing this dispensation.

---

[8] Ryrie, Charles. 52-53

5. The Dispensation of Mosaic Law. This is where the law is delivered to the people, and the people fail again and again to follow the commandments. Pestilence, wanderings, and captivities reward them. This dispensation has the most scripture attached to it. See Exodus 19:1-John 14:30.

6. The Dispensation of Grace. This is the present dispensation. Ephesians 2:8-9 truly define this dispensation; "For by grace you have been saved through faith; and that not of yourselves, it is the gift of God; not as a result of works, so that no one may boast.." The majority of the New Testament is contained within this dispensation, carrying all the way from Acts 2:1 to revelation 20:1-15.

7. The Dispensation of the Millennium. This is the period after the Second Advent of Christ, when He will reign for a thousand years.

Name	Scripture	Responsibilities	Judgment(s)
Innocency	Genesis 1:3-3:6	Keep Garden Do not eat one fruit	Curses; and physical and spiritual death
Conscience	Genesis 3:7-8:14	Do good	Flood
Civil Government	Genesis 8:15-11:9	Fill earth Capital punishment	Forced scattering by confusion of languages
Patriarchal Rule	Genesis 11:10-Exodus 18-27	Stay in Promised Land Believe and obey God	Egyptian bondage and wilderness wanderings
Mosaic Law	Exodus 19:1-John 14:30	Keep the law Walk with God	Captivities
Grace	Acts 2:1-Revelation 19:21	Believe on Christ Walk with Christ	Death Loss of rewards
Millennium	Revelation 20:1-15	Believe and obey Christ and His government	Death Great White Throne Judgment

Table 1: The Dispensations[9]

It must again be emphasized that there is much more to dispensationalism then this list of dispensations. It is necessary

---

[9] Ryrie, Charles. 54

at this point to examine the two major viewpoints within evangelical Christianity. What follows are definitions of Dispensational and Covenantal theology. Dr. Paul Enns defines Dispensational Theology as follows:

> Dispensationalism is a system of interpretation that seeks to establish a unity in the Scriptures through its central focus on the grace of God. Although dispensationalists recognize differing stewardships or dispensations whereby man was put under a trust by the Lord, they teach that response to God's revelation in each dispensation is by faith (salvation is *always* by grace through faith). Dispensationalists arrive at their system of interpretation through two primary principles: (1) maintaining a consistently literal method of interpretation, and (2) maintaining a distinction between Israel and the church.[10]

While I essentially agree with Dr. Enns' definition, I think that it is important to recognize that, while dispensationalism may be a system, it must be understood that going into ANY study of the Bible with preconceptions is *eisegesis*, and should be avoided. Remember Kahler's maxim, quoted earlier. A dispensational belief is the result of a consistent hermeneutic, not the cause thereof.

A dispensationalist is one who would insist on less allegory within scripture. Of course, most covenantalists would argue that they insist on maintaining a consistently literal method of interpretation. It is just that they get a little fuzzy when determining what is, and what is not, allegory. Dr. Enns defines Covenant theology as follows:

---

[10] Enns, Paul. *The Moody Handbook of Theology.* 513

> Covenant theology is a system of interpreting the Scriptures on the basis of two covenants: the covenant of works and the covenant of grace. Some covenant theologians specify three covenants: works, redemption, and grace. Covenant theology teaches that God initially made a covenant of works with Adam, promising eternal life for obedience and death for disobedience. Adam failed, and death entered the human race. God, however, moved to resolve man's dilemma by entering into a covenant of grace through which the problem of sin and death would be overcome. Christ is the ultimate mediator of God's covenant of grace.[11]

In the past it was much easier to distinguish between the major schools of thought. But today the lines are not as distinct as they once were. Covenant theologians are not anxious to go on record as being adherents of the allegorical method. When asked, they will argue that they are also support a literal hermeneutic. But where a dispensationalist will seek to interpret scripture literally, unless it is clearly allegorical, the covenantalists will insist that a larger amount of scripture IS allegorical. Especially in the area of eschatology.

So it can be seen that dispensation is not a stand-alone doctrine. Its aspects boil over into all of the other areas of theology, but especially in the areas of soteriology, eschatology, and ecclesiology. Each of the doctrines named will contain a discussion of the dispensational aspects within their respective chapters.

---

[11] Enns, Paul. 503

Theology Proper & Trintarianism
Chapter Three

God exists. He always has, and he always will. He is transcendent. That is, He is separate from his creation. For proof of this fact, see Genesis 1:1.

> [1]In the beginning God created the heavens and the earth.

Attributes of God

God's attributes show that he is infinite, He is perfect, and he is the source of everything in the universe. He created the universe *Ex Nihlo*, that is, out of nothing. And while everything else has a beginning, God alone is truly eternal. He has no beginning, and will never end. His attributes include:

1. Sufficiency. God is totally and absolutely complete within himself. See Exodus 3:14:

    > [14]And God said to Moses, "I AM WHO I AM." And He said, "Thus you shall say to the children of Israel, 'I AM has sent me to you.'"

2. Eternality. God is without beginning or end. He is free from all time measurements and is Himself the ultimate source of time. The following scriptures demonstrate this principle:

    > [2]Before the mountains were brought forth, Or ever You had formed the earth and the world, Even from everlasting to everlasting, You are God.
    >
    > - Psalms 90:2

    > [25] To God our Savior, Who alone is wise, Be glory and majesty, Dominion and power, Both now and forever. Amen.
    >
    > - Jude 25

3. Transcendence. God is independent of His creation. For evidence, See Acts 17:22-25.

4. Holiness. This is the quality that separates God from all that is wicked. God is eternally pure. The following scriptures demonstrate this principle:

> [11]"Who is like You, O LORD, among the gods? Who is like You, glorious in holiness, Fearful in praises, doing wonders?
> -Exodus 15:11

> [16]because it is written, "Be holy, for I am holy."
> -1 Peter 1:16

5. Immutability. God is unchangeable. He is the same today, yesterday, and tomorrow. The following scriptures demonstrate this principle:

   > [27]But You *are* the same, And Your years will have no end.
   > -Psalms 102:27

   > [8]Jesus Christ *is* the same yesterday, today, and forever.
   > -Hebrews 13:8

6. Infinite. God is not limited as human are. He has no boundaries or limits.

   > [1]Thus says the LORD, "Heaven is My throne and the earth is My footstool. Where then is a house you could build for Me? And where is a place that I may rest?
   > - Isaiah 66:1

7. Love. This attribute is characterized by God's giving of Himself for the benefit of others. See John 3:16 for a demonstration of this principle:

   > [16]"For God so loved the world, that He gave His only begotten Son, that whoever believes in Him shall not perish, but have eternal life.

8. Omnipotence. God possesses the ability to do all things, which are consistent with His character.

> [27]"Behold, I am the LORD, the God of all flesh; is anything too difficult for Me?"
> - Jeremiah 32:27

> [26]And looking at *them* Jesus said to them, "With people this is impossible, but with God all things are possible."
> - Matthew 19:26

9. Omnipresence. God is everywhere at once. He accomplishes this without diffusing, expanding, multiplying, or dividing Himself. He simply is. See the following scriptures for a demonstration:

> [7]Where can I go from Your Spirit? Or where can I flee from Your presence?
> - Psalms 139:7

> [24]"The God who made the world and all things in it, since He is Lord of heaven and earth, does not dwell in temples made with hands
> - Acts 17:24

10. Omniscience. God is all knowing. For evidence, see the following scriptures:

> [4]He counts the number of the stars; He gives names to all of them.
> - Psalms 147:4

> [13] And there is no creature hidden from His sight, but all things are open and laid bare to the eyes of Him with whom we have to do.
> - Hebrews 4:13

11. Righteousness. God is the perfect standard. He is righteous to the point of not being able to tolerate sin. 1 Peter 1:16 says:

    > [16] because it is written, "YOU SHALL BE HOLY, FOR I AM HOLY."

12. Sovereignty. God's sovereignty concerns His absolute control over all of His creation. The following scriptures demonstrate this principle:

    > [13] "But He is unique and who can turn Him? And *what* His soul desires, that He does.
    > - Job 23:13

    > [11] also we have obtained an inheritance, having been predestined according to His purpose who works all things after the counsel of His will,
    > - Ephesians 1:11

13. Truthful. God is truth. He cannot lie, and therefore cannot be deceived. The following scriptures are evidence of this important attribute of God.

    > [16] Because he who is blessed in the earth will be blessed by the God of truth; And he who swears in the earth will swear by the God of truth; Because the former troubles are forgotten, And because they are hidden from My sight!
    > - Isaiah 65:16

> [9](for the fruit of the Light *consists* in all goodness and righteousness and truth), [10]trying to learn what is pleasing to the Lord.
>
> — Ephesians 5:9-10

14. Just. God's holiness requires that punishment be dealt out for sin. The following scriptures demonstrate this principle:

> [6]Then the LORD passed by in front of him and proclaimed, "The LORD, the LORD God, compassionate and gracious, slow to anger, and abounding in lovingkindness and truth; [7]who keeps lovingkindness for thousands, who forgives iniquity, transgression and sin; yet He will by no means leave *the guilty* unpunished, visiting the iniquity of fathers on the children and on the grandchildren to the third and fourth generations."
>
> — Exodus 34:6-7

> [31]because He has fixed a day in which He will judge the world in righteousness through a Man whom He has appointed, having furnished proof to all men by raising Him from the dead."
>
> — Acts 17:31

No one of God's attributes is ever separated from the others. That is God is one hundred percent Love. He is one hundred percent righteous, etc. None of these qualities conflict with one another. They are inherent with the personality of God.

Doctrine of the Trinity

> Glory be to the Father, and to the Son and to the Holy Ghost. As it was in the beginning, is now, and ever shall be. World without end, Amen.[12]

> Praise God from whom All blessings flow. Praise Him all creatures hers below. Praise Him all above, ye heavenly host. Praise Father, Son and Holy Ghost.[13]

Although virtually all true Christians base their faith on the foundation of the doctrine of the Trinity, it can not be found (by name, at any rate) anywhere in either the New or Old Testaments. It is implicit, rather than explicit. Although even the youngest child, fresh from Sunday school can recite the Doxology, even the most mature, most scholarly adult has difficulty in understanding this most complex doctrine.

Historically the word Trinity was not used by the early church, and indeed, was not used at all until the 2nd century, when it was coined by Tertullian. He was also the first to use the term Person as representative of the three aspects of the one God. You may remember Tertullian as the man who said "What has Athens to Say to Jerusalem?" In this respect he rejected Greek philosophy, and became the first anti-philosophical philosopher. It is somewhat ironic that he is remembered as a philosopher at all! However, he adapted the Latin term Trinitas from the Greek word Trias, which was already being used. It was at the Council of Nicaea, held in 325 AD, that the doctrine was officially adopted as the position of the Church. Succeeding councils subsequently upheld it.

---

[12] Gloria Patri, Original source for the words unknown, dating from the 2nd Century. The original tune is from an old Scottish Chant. *Worship and Service Hymnal*.

[13] *Doxology*, Thomas Ken, Louis Bougeois. *Worship and Service Hymnal*.

Since it has been stated earlier in this paper that the doctrine of the trinity is implicit rather than explicit, it is necessary to discuss 1 John 5:7. Always remember, a major doctrine should never be based upon a questionable text! In the original King James, 1 John 5:7 reads as follows:

> For there are three that bear record in heaven, the Father, the Word, and the Holy Ghost: and these three are one.

In his book *the letters of John and Jude*, Barclay says the following about this Controversial verse:

> "The revised Version omits this verse, and does not even mention it in the margin, and none of the newer translations includes it. It is quite certain that it does not belong to the original text. The facts are as follows. First, it does not occur in any Greek manuscript earlier than the 14th century. The great manuscripts belong to the 3rd and 4th centuries, and it occurs in none of them. None of the great early fathers of the Church knew it. The first person to quote it was a Spanish heretic called Priscillian. Thereafter it crept gradually into the Latin texts of the New Testament although, as we have seen, it did not gain an entry into the Greek manuscripts.
> How then did it get into the text? Originally it must have been a scribal gloss or comment in the margin. Since it seemed to offer good scriptural evidence for the doctrine of the Trinity, through time it came to be accepted by theologians as part of the text, especially in those early days of scholarship before the great manuscripts were discovered.

But how did it last, and how did it come to be in the Authorized Version? The first Greek testament to be published was that of Erasmus in1516. Erasmus was a great scholar and, knowing that this verse was not in the original text, he did not include it in his first edition. By this time, however, theologians were using the verse. It had, for instance, been printed in the Latin Vulgate of 1514. Erasmus was therefore criticized for omitting it. His answer was that if anyone could show him a Greek manuscript which had the words in it, he would print them in his next edition. Someone did produce a very late and very bad text in which the word did occur in Greek; and Erasmus, true to his word, printed the verse in his 1522 edition. The next step was that in 1550 Stephanus printed his great edition of the Greek New Testament. This 1550 edition of Stephanus was called-he gave it that name himself-[14]The Received Text, and it was the basis of the Authorized Version and of the Greek text for centuries to come. That is how this verse got into the Authorized Version. There is, of course, nothing wrong with it; but modern scholarship has made it quite certain that John did not write it and that it is a much later commentary on, and addition to, his words; and that is why all modern translations omit it."

To which manuscripts was Dr. Barclay referring? Using the critical apparatus of the United Bible Societies *Greek New Testament*, it was determined that the manuscripts in question were 221mg and 2318. These are miniscules[15] and are normally cited only when they are of special significance for certain variants." The "mg" that has been tacked onto 221 signifies

---

[14] Textus Receptus
[15] United Bible Societies; *The Greek New Testament*, xx

[16]"textual evidence contained in the margin of a manuscript." The interesting thing about these miniscules is that neither of them contain 1 John! Miniscule 221 dates from the 10th century, and contains fragments of Acts and of Paul's Epistles. Miniscule 2318 dates from the 14th century, and contains pieces of the book of Acts. The miniscules in question were probably marginal notes, or references from one epistle to another. Much as Bible student's today write notes in the margins, or look up cross references in modern study Bibles.

At this point, let us return to scripture. We begin with the Old Testament, in the book of Deuteronomy. Chapter 6, verse 4 tells us:

Hear O Israel the Lord is our God, the Lord is one.

שְׁמַע יִשְׂרָאֵל יְיָ אֱלֹהֵינוּ יְיָ אֶחָד:

Shema Yisrael YHWH   Elohanu   YHWH   Echad
               (Adonai)   (Adonai)

Table 2. *The Shema*

From this we can logically infer that God is one. Or can we? Because the word for God used in this verse is the plural form of the word *Elohim [Elahanu]* we can also infer that, while God is indeed one, he is also more than one. How can this be? How can one be more than one. I do not know. But since the scripture says that it is so, I believe that it is so. How important is this verse? To the Jews it is of utmost importance. It is the foundation upon which the rest of Judaism rests. Here is an excerpt taken from the *Sabbath and Festival Prayer Book*, published by the Rabbinical Assembly of America:

---

[16] United Bible Societies; xxvii

> "The Shema is the most important prayer in the Jewish liturgy. With the Shema upon their lips, Martyrs in every age, including our own, have died for the sanctification of God's name and the glory of Israel. It's words are the very last spoken by pious men of every age, and it's sacred syllables the first taught to little children. It is a central feature of the morning and evening service and is recited before retiring at night."[17]

So we can see how important the verse is to the Jewish People. But it is important for Christians as well. Because it gives us a clue about the complex nature of God's person/s. And so, with our first clue directing our progress, lets move on to the second! To quote Sir Arthur Conan Doyle, "The Games afoot!"

> And God said, let Us make man in Our image, after Our likeness.
> - Genesis 1:26

Either God is using the royal "Us" and "Our", which he is certainly qualified to do, or He is conversing among his persons. It is always best to interpret the passage according to its plainest, most ordinary meaning. Earlier in this paper this writer quoted Dr. David L. Cooper's Golden Rule of Interpretation, and will do so again:

> "When the plain sense of Scripture makes common sense, seek no other sense; therefore, take every word at its primary, ordinary, usual, literal meaning unless the facts of the immediate context, studied in the light of related passages and axiomatic and fundamental truths, indicate clearly otherwise.[18]"

---

[17] *Sabbath and Festival Prayer Book.* 238
[18] Garland Shinn; *Practical Biblical Hermeneutics.* 7

The context of the verse, as well as that of the verses that precedes and follow, clearly indicate that God is conversing among his persons. Genesis 3:22 tells us:

> And the Lord God said, the man has become as
> one of us, to know good and evil.

No question here. The verse does not say has become as I, but clearly uses the plural. Once again, the "Golden Rule" clearly indicates the plurality of God. Leaving the Book of Genesis, let us turn to Isaiah 6:8a, which tells us:

> Then I heard the voice of the Lord saying,
> "Whom shall I send for Us?"

Again, the Lord, in his own words refers to Himself in the plural form. [19]Ryrie's notes on the verse say "God is seen as a King in council. This phrase certainly allows for the fuller NT revelation of the Trinity."

The problem with Old Testament Scripture as applied to the doctrine of Trinity is that, although it clearly shows the plurality, it is not specific in enough about God's triune aspects. This is not a problem for evangelical Christians, but does open the door for arguments by Unitarians, Moslems, and the various cults.

And now let us progress to the New Testament. The scripture here is clearer about the various aspects of God's persons. We will begin with John, chapter 1, verses 1-3:

> In the beginning was the Word, and the Word
> was With Go, and the Word was God. He was in
> the beginning with God. All things came into

---

[19] *Ryrie Study Bible.* 1057

being through Him, and apart from Him nothing
came into being that has come into being.

While this verses, like verse previously quoted, does not use the word trinity explicitly, it does much more than imply that God's persons are more than one. It tells us specifically that Jesus was God. It tells us specifically that before the world was created, Jesus existed. The verses tell us that, indeed, Jesus IS God. But it also tells us that He was with God. The word used in Greek in this verse for "Word" is *Logos*. This word means "word, thought, concept, and the expressions thereof."[20] To the Greek mentality, *Logos* suggests the ideas of creative expression and control. The *Logos* as applied to Jesus speaks of His creative qualities. He is God, and yet is distinct from God. Jesus tells us, in John 17:24 that He was with the Father before the creation of the world.

"Father, I desire that they also, whom You have given Me, be with me where I am, so that they may see My glory which you have given Me, for You loved me before the foundation of the world.

In these verses two of the three divine persons are clearly shown. Anyone arguing that Jesus was not God has not, or will not, understood the first three verses of John. And lest anyone question whether the *Logos* is Jesus Himself, continue on to the next verse, John 1:14;

And the Word became flesh, and dwelt among us, and we saw His glory, glory as of the only begotten from the Father, full of grace and truth.

That refers to Jesus. Preceding verses have demonstrated His divinity, and here is shown His humanity. Scripture teaches that God is a being of spirit. See John 4, Verse 24:

---

[20] *Ryrie Study Bible.* 1679

> God is spirit, and those who worship Him must worship in spirit and truth.

Scripture also teaches that Jesus dwelt among us as a human being. Notice that I did not use the word "person". This is because God is spirit, and yet has the necessary attributes of a person. Tony Evans says the following in his book *Our God is Awesome:*

> "God is a person. When I say this, I mean that He has the three attributes of personhood: emotions or feelings, intellect or the mind, and will or the power to choose. Those three things make people distinct from the rest of creation. God is a Person because He feels, thinks, and chooses."[21]

So, God is both Spirit and Human. When speaking here of spirit, the reference is to God's essence, not to the Third Person of the Trinity. Up to this point two of Gods persons have been demonstrated. Now to show the Third Person of the Trinity.

Once again, let us begin at the beginning. John tells us that Jesus was with the father at the creation of the world. Genesis 1:2 tells us that the spirit was also present.

> The earth was formless and void, and darkness was over the surface of the deep, and the Spirit of God was moving over the surface of the waters.

In his excellent book *Basic Theology*, Dr. Ryrie asserts that there are seven verses that speak of the Holy Spirit's work in creation. In addition to Genesis 1:2, he lists Job 26:13, 27:3 and 33:4; Psalms 33:6 and 104:30; and Isaiah 40:12-14. Of these

---

[21] Evans, Tony. *Our God is Awesome.* 43

verses, only the aforementioned Genesis 1:2, Psalms 104:30, and the middle verse of Isaiah would seem to refer to the Third Person of the trinity. Job 26:13 tells us:

> By His breath the heavens are cleared; His hand
> has pierced the fleeing serpent.

The same verse in the KJV reads a little differently:

> By his spirit he hath garnished the heavens; his
> hand hath formed the crooked serpent.

The word is question is *Ruach*. It means breath, wind, spirit. It can be translated spirit, but has been generally construed to mean breath. Turning back for a moment to Genesis 1:2, the word used for spirit here is also Ruach! So why is it translated as Spirit in one and breath in another. Once again we have to turn to David Cooper's Golden rule of interpretation. The verse in Genesis seems to refer to God's Spirit literally moving over the surface of the waters. Job is speaking figuratively, using anthropomorphism. We know that God does not really have breath. Job is glorifying God by pointing out his majesty. It is a beautiful, poetic expression. But do not forget that Job is classified as a poetic book. Genesis is a history, pure and simple.

> You send forth Your Spirit, they are created; and
> You renew the face of the ground.
> - Psalms 104:30

Ryrie's notes tell us that this verse tells of the spirit of every living thing depending on the Spirit of God.[22]

> Who has directed the Spirit of the Lord, or as
> His counselor has informed Him?
> - Isaiah 40:13

---
[22] *Ryrie Study Bible*, page 926

Once again, the word translated as Spirit is *Ruach*. A pretty versatile word! So it can be proven that the Spirit participated in creation. But where else was it active?

> The Spirit of the Lord spoke by me, and His word was on my tongue.
> - 2 Samuel 23:2

> On the other hand I am filled with power-With the Spirit of the Lord-And with justice and courage to make known to Jacob his rebellious act, even to Israel his sin.
> -Micah 3:8

So it is obvious that another function of the Holy Spirit in the Old Testament was assist the Prophets. This should come as no surprise. The primary function of the Prophets was to communicate God's word to His people. What better aspect of His person than that of the Holy Spirit? So the Spirit participated in creation, and directed the actions and words of the Prophets. All this occurred in the Old Testament. But what about His work in the next dispensation? John 15:26 helps answer this question:

> "When the Helper comes, whom I will send to you from the Father, that is, the Spirit of the father, He will bear witness of me,"

> "But when He, the Spirit of truth, comes, He will guide you into all truth; for He will not speak on His own initiative, but whatever He hears He will speak, and He will disclose to you what is to come."
> - John 16:1

So here Jesus tells us that when He has left, He will send a helper to guide us. In the Old Testament it was similar, but not as personal. The Spirit directed the Prophets, and the people would be influenced by the word of God. Now the Spirit would directly affect each individual believer. But is this Spirit the same as the Old Testament Spirit. Scripture clearly tells us that He is! For an example, see Acts 28:25-27.

> And when they did not agree with one another, they began leaving after Paul had spoken one parting word, "The Holy Spirit rightly spoke through Isaiah the prophet to your fathers, saying, 'GO TO THIS PEOPLE AND SAY, YOU WILL KEEP ON HEARING, BUT WILL NOT UNDERSTAND, AND YOU WILL KEEP ON SEEING, BUT WILL NOT PERCIEVE; FOR THE HEART OF THIS PEOPLE HAS BECOME DULL, AND WITH THEIR EARS THEY SCARCELY HEAR, AND THEY HAVE CLOSED THEIR EYES; OTHERWISE THEY MIGHT SEE WITH THEIR EYES, AND HEAR WITH THEIR EARS, AND UNDERSTAND WITH THEIR HEART AND RETURN, AND I WOULD HEAL THEM.'"

Here is the ultimate scriptural proof that the Spirit of the Old was indeed the Spirit of the New! So the scripture teaches that the Spirit is distinct from the Father and distinct from the son. Observe the following illustration, taken from Ryrie's Basic Theology:

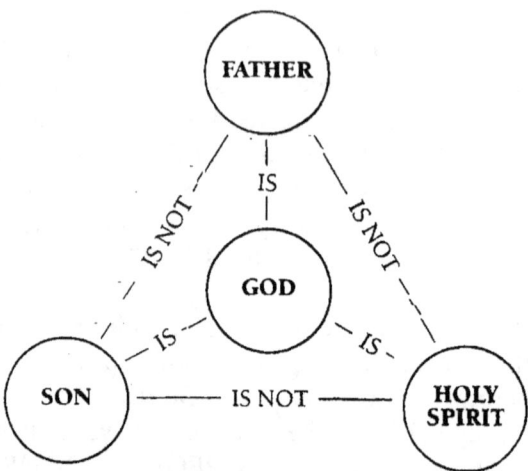

Table 3: Ryrie's Trinitarian model

While there are no perfect illustrations of this doctrine, this seems to be the best. The three persons of the trinity are each totally God. The Father is one hundred percent God. The Son is one hundred percent God. And the Spirit is one Hundred percent God. Each of the person's of the trinity are distinct from the other. That the Father is God has never been seriously questioned. Christian's, Moslem's, Unitarians, whatever the creed or denomination will acknowledge the Deity of the Father. Many groups have questioned the Deity of Jesus, but scripture clearly proves what some would deny. Many groups have also challenged the Deity of the Holy Spirit. These groups would relegate Him to being a part of either the father or the Son. That is to say that he is the result of the Deities actions, rather than the source of the actions. This position is illogical when faced with the amount of scripture that supports the ministry of the Holy Spirit. In addition, Ryrie asserts, through scripture, that the Holy Spirit Possesses and Exhibits the Attributes of a person, as described by Tony Evans. In Chapter 59 of Basic Theology, Ryrie has the following to say:

1. He has intelligence. He knows and searches the things of God. See 1 Corinthians 2:10-11.

2. He possesses a mind. See Romans 8:27.

3. He is able to teach people. See 1 Corinthians 2:13.

4. He also directs the activities of Christians. See Acts 16:6-11.

Since genuine personality possesses intelligence, feelings, and will, and since the Spirit has these attributes, He must be a person.

And so, to use a phrase of the bard from Henry V, "It is clear as the summer's sun" that the Spirit was, is, and will always be a Divine Person of the One. And as if the evidence already presented is not sufficient, let us turn to the venerable Calvin, from Chapter XIII of His *Institutes*.

> "On the other hand, the scriptures demonstrate that there is some distinction between the Father and the Word, the Word and the Spirit; but the magnitude of the mystery reminds us of the great reverence and soberness which ought to be employed in discussing it. ... Therefore, let us beware of imagining such a Trinity of persons as will distract our thoughts, instead of brining them instantly back to the unity. The words, Father, Son, and Holy Spirit, certainly indicate a real distinction, not allowing us to suppose that they are merely epithets by which God is variously designated from His works. Still, they indicate distinction only, not division. ... Christ intimates the distinction between the Holy Spirit

and the Father, when He says that the Spirit proceedeth from the Father, and between the Holy Spirit and himself, when he speaks of him as another, as he does when he declares that he will send another Comforter;"

Calvin goes on to observe the following Distinctions:

"That to the Father is attributed the beginning of action, the fountain and source of all things; to the Son, wisdom, counsel, and arrangement in action, while the energy and efficacy of action is assigned to the Spirit,"

In summary; the Trinity was a mystery to the great theologians Calvin and Luther. It is a mystery to the great theologians of our time. The arguments presented in this chapter have been drawn from a variety of sources; scriptural, philosophical, and theological. The concept is difficult for humans to comprehend, because the God that it represents is Awesome in scope. If He were not, then He would not be Himself. Trinitarian doctrine has been held as truth since the third century, and, along with the Deity of Christ, separates Christians from cultists.

Christology
Chapter Four

Jesus has existed eternally. He was in the beginning, and is the second person of the trinity. The following scriptures demonstrate this principle:

> ¹In the beginning was the Word, and the Word was with God, and the Word was God. ²He was in the beginning with God.
> - John 1:1-2

> ⁵⁸Jesus said to them, "Most assuredly, I say to you, before Abraham was, I AM." ⁵⁹Then they took up stones to throw at Him; but Jesus hid Himself and went out of the temple, going through the midst of them, and so passed by.
> - John 8:58-59

> ⁵And now, O Father, glorify Me together with Yourself, with the glory which I had with You before the world was.
>
> - John 17:5

He has neither beginning nor end. Jesus is eternal, as only God can be. Man is finite. He will die physically, but spiritually, will live forever. The difference is in the beginning. Man was created; Jesus has always existed.

Jesus claimed divinity for himself. It is difficult for many to accept this, but it is true nonetheless. John 8:58 needs to be looked at in greater detail. There are hundreds of thousands of "Christians" in America who believe that Jesus never claimed to be God, but was "only" the son of God. This verse proves that this is simply not so. The problem stems from the difference between the meaning of *I AM* in English and the original languages. In John 8:58, Ryrie's notes connect the verse with Exodus 3:14.

> ¹⁴And God said to Moses, "I AM WHO I AM." And He said, "Thus you shall say to the children of Israel, 'I AM has sent me to you.

Even when referring back to Exodus, the reader can become confused. What exactly is the meaning of *I Am*? Leaving aside, for the moment, the meaning in Hebrew, lets look at the passage in Greek.

> ⁵⁸ εἶπεν αὐτοῖς ᾿Ιησοῦς, ᾿Αμὴν ἀμὴν λέγω ὑμῖν, πρὶν ᾿Αβραὰμ γενέσθαι ἐγὼ εἰμί.
> - John 8:58 (Critical text)

The Septuagint uses the same construction in Exodus 3:14. This clearly demonstrates that from the Greek, the construction is the same. The authors of the LXX translated the ineffable name of God as "I AM". So Jesus was really saying, *before Abraham was, Yahweh*. The Jews knew this, as evidenced by verse 59, where they tried to stone Him. Make no mistake, Jesus claimed divinity.

Jesus is equal in person with the father. The following scripture demonstrates this important principle:

> [9]Jesus said to him, "Have I been with you so long, and yet you have not known Me, Philip? He who has seen Me has seen the Father; so how can you say, 'Show us the Father'? [10]Do you not believe that I am in the Father, and the Father in Me? The words that I speak to you I do not speak on My own *authority;* but the Father who dwells in Me does the works. [11]Believe Me that I *am* in the Father and the Father in Me, or else believe Me for the sake of the works themselves.
> - John 14:9-11

Jesus possessed both human and Divine nature's. Jesus became human, and existed as the God-man. As such, he possessed two natures, being both human and divine. The union of these two natures was accomplished by the supernatural Conception by the Holy Spirit using the Virgin Mary. In addition to the scripture presented below, see the following for evidence: Matthew 1:18-25, Luke 1:28-35, John 1:14, and Hebrews 10:5.

> [14]Therefore the Lord Himself will give you a sign: Behold, the virgin shall conceive and bear a Son, and shall call His name Immanuel.
> - Isaiah 7:14

Jesus led a perfect life. An important aspect of Jesus' purity, is that, in spite of the fact that he had a human mother, he was preserved from original sin. Scripture informs us that He lived a sinless life, perfect in all respects. In addition to the scripture presented, see the following for additional verification: Luke 1:35, Hebrews 4:15, and 1 Peter 1:19.

> [21]For He made Him who knew no sin to be sin for us, that we might become the righteousness of God in Him.
> -2 Corinthians 5:21

Jesus did not give up Divinity. As the God-man, Jesus did not relinquish Deity. He chose to be subject to the will of the First and Third Person of the trinity, the father and Holy Spirit. The following scripture demonstrates this principle:

> [5]Let this mind be in you which was also in Christ Jesus, [6]who, being in the form of God, did not consider it robbery to be equal with God, [7]but made Himself of no reputation, taking the form of a bondservant, *and* coming in the likeness of men. [8]And being found in appearance as a man, He humbled Himself and became obedient to *the point of* death, even the death of the cross.
> - Philippians 2:5-8

In summary, Jesus' death on the cross was a voluntary, substitutionary death, the Just for the unjust. His death satisfied the demands of God's holiness. Because it is written:

> Without the shedding of blood there can be no remission of sin.
> - Hebrews 9:22

Jesus' death alone is the basis for reconciliation and redemption.

Pneumatology
Chapter Five

The Personality of the Holy Spirit

The Holy Spirit is the third person of the trinity. He is equal with both the father and the Son. He possesses the same attributes as the other persons. In scripture, He is called God. As evidence, see Acts 5:3-4:

> [3]But Peter said, "Ananias, why has Satan filled your heart to lie to the Holy Spirit and keep back part of the price of the land for yourself? [4]While it remained, was it not your own? And after it was sold, was it not in your own control? Why have you conceived this thing in your heart? You have not lied to men but to God."

He is accounted as equal with other persons of the trinity. See the following scripture:

> [19] Go therefore and make disciples of all the nations, baptizing them in the name of the Father and of the Son and of the Holy Spirit,
> - Matthew 28:19

The Attributes of the Holy Spirit

He possesses the same attributes as God.

1. Omnipresence. See Psalms 139:7 for a demonstration of this principle:

   > [7] Where can I go from Your Spirit? Or where can I flee from Your presence?

2. Omnipotence. As evidence of this principle, see Luke 1:35:

   > [35] And the angel answered and said to her, "The Holy Spirit will come upon you, and the power of the Highest will overshadow you; therefore, also, that Holy One who is to be born will be called the Son of God.

3. Omniscience. 1 Corinthians 2:10 demonstrates this principle:

   > [10] But God has revealed them to us through His Spirit. For the Spirit searches all things, yes, the deep things of God.

4. He was active in the works of creation. See Genesis 1:2:

> [2]The earth was without form, and void; and darkness was on the face of the deep. And the Spirit of God was hovering over the face of the waters.

5. He receives Honor due God. As evidence, see 1 Corinthians 3:16:

> [16]Do you not know that you are the temple of God and that the Spirit of God dwells in you? [17]If anyone defiles the temple of God, God will destroy him. For the temple of God is holy, which temple you are.

Personality Traits of the Holy Spirit

He has the three traits that are necessary for personality.

1. Intellect. As evidence, see the following scripture:

> [27]Now He who searches the hearts knows what the mind of the Spirit is, because He makes intercession for the saints according to the will of God.
>
> -Romans 8:27

2. Will. The following scriptures demonstrate this aspect:

> [2]As they ministered to the Lord and fasted, the Holy Spirit said, "Now separate to Me Barnabas and Saul for the work to which I have called them."
>
> - Acts 13:2

3. Emotion. For a scriptural demonstration of this aspect, see Isaiah 63:8-11.

The ministries of the Holy Spirit

1. Conviction and restraint. One of the ministries of the Holy Spirit is to convict unbelievers of sin, righteousness, and judgment. Until the rapture of the saints, the Holy Spirit restrains evil in the world, as evidenced by the following scriptures:

> ^{8}And when He has come, He will convict the world of sin, and of righteousness, and of judgment: ^{9}of sin, because they do not believe in Me; ^{10}of righteousness, because I go to My Father and you see Me no more; ^{11}of judgment, because the ruler of this world is judged.
> –John 16:8-11

> ^{7}For the mystery of lawlessness is already at work; only He who now restrains will do so until He is taken out of the way.
> -2 Thessalonians 2:7

2. Regenerating the unregenerate as they believe. For evidence, see Titus 3:5

> ^{5}not by works of righteousness which we have done, but according to His mercy He saved us, through the washing of regeneration and renewing of the Holy Spirit,

3. Baptism of the spirit. Baptism of believers into the body of Christ at conversion. 1 Corinthians 12:13 demonstrates this well:

> [13]For by one Spirit we were all baptized into one body—whether Jews or Greeks, whether slaves or free—and have all been made to drink into one Spirit.

4. The permanent indwelling of the believer at conversion. See the following scripture for a demonstration of this principle:

   > [19]Or do you not know that your body is the temple of the Holy Spirit who is in you, whom you have from God, and you are not your own?
   > - 1 Corinthians 6:19

5. The sealing of the believer at conversion

   > [13]In Him you also trusted, after you heard the word of truth, the gospel of your salvation; in whom also, having believed, you were sealed with the Holy Spirit of promise,
   > - Ephesians 1:13

6. The filling of the believer at conversion.

   > [52]And the disciples were filled with joy and with the Holy Spirit.
   > - Acts 13:52

   > [18]And do not be drunk with wine, in which is dissipation; but be filled with the Spirit,
   > - Ephesians 5:18

7. Illumination of the believers mind to understand the scriptures.

> [12] Now we have received, not the spirit of the world, but the Spirit who is from God, that we might know the things that have been freely given to us by God. [13] These things we also speak, not in words which man's wisdom teaches but which the Holy Spirit teaches, comparing spiritual things with spiritual. [14] But the natural man does not receive the things of the Spirit of God, for they are foolishness to him; nor can he know them, because they are spiritually discerned.
>
> -1 Corinthians 2:12-14

This scripture demonstrates the difference between the saved and the unsaved. The believer is able to comprehend the things of the spirit, whereas, to the unregenerate, these same things appear as foolishness. All who came to belief as adults have seen this principle demonstrated. Friends are unable to understand the changes in behavior. Since they see nothing wrong with their lifestyles, they see the believer, their former companion, as prudish, foolish, and self-righteous!

8. The continual leading and guiding of the believer. For evidence of this important ministry, see Acts 16:6-10.

9. Assurance of Salvation.

> [13] These things I have written to you who believe in the name of the Son of God, that you may know that you have eternal life, and that you may continue to believe in the name of the Son of God.
>
> - 1 John 5:13

10. Intercession for the believer

> ²⁶Likewise the Spirit also helps in our weaknesses. For we do not know what we should pray for as we ought, but the Spirit Himself makes intercession for us with groanings which cannot be uttered.
> - Romans 8:26

11. Empowering the believer for acts of service

> ³¹And when they had prayed, the place where they were assembled together was shaken; and they were all filled with the Holy Spirit, and they spoke the word of God with boldness.
> - Acts 4:31

The Holy Spirit and Spiritual Gifts

The word of God teaches that the Holy Spirit bestows spiritual gifts upon individual believers in this age for the purpose of edification. I believe that some of the gifts bestowed in the early church were temporary and were to serve until the completion of the New Testament scriptures. Other gifts continued for the purpose of building up the local church until the rapture of the church.

Aspects of Spiritual Gifts

1. The Holy Spirit is sovereign in His bestowal of spiritual gifts. For example, see the following scriptures, 1 Corinthians 12:8-11; Ephesians 4:11-12.

2. Some spiritual gifts are temporary. Apostles and prophets served only to lay the foundation of the Church. One of the criteria to be an apostle was to be with Christ during His earthly ministry. The only exception was Paul, and possibly James. In addition to the scripture that follows, see Acts 1:21-22; 1 Corinthians 15:8, and Galatians 1:19.

> [20]having been built on the foundation of the apostles and prophets, Jesus Christ Himself being the chief cornerstone, [21]in whom the whole building, being fitted together, grows into a holy temple in the Lord,
>
> — Ephesians 2:20-22

Biblical evidence points to the fact that the gifts of prophecy, tongues and their interpretation have ceased. All revelatory gifts, along with vindicating sign-gifts such as healing, raising of the dead and "wholesale" miracles would become unnecessary after the completion of the New Testament.

> [8]Love never fails. But whether there are prophecies, they will fail; whether there are tongues, they will cease; whether there is knowledge, it will vanish away. [9]For we know in part and we prophesy in part. [10]But when that which is perfect has come, then that which is in part will be done away. [11]When I was a child, I spoke as a child, I understood as a child, I thought as a child; but when I became a man, I put away childish things. [12]For now we see in a mirror, dimly, but then face to face. Now I know in part, but then I shall know just as I also am known.
>
> — 1 Corinthians 13:8-11

This passage has been misinterpreted to mean that there is actually a spiritual language, a language of angels, which can be spoken by believers. There is no evidence in scripture that such a language is available to believers. It is used primarily among the charismatic Churches to justify "glossalalia", that is, the practice of a believer to babble in an unrecognizable tongue, a spiritual tongue of angels, in order to satisfy their belief that one must speak in tongues in order to demonstrate their salvation. These well meaning Christians have completely misunderstood the words of Paul. He is saying, "If I speak...And have not love." The passage is about love. He is not saying that he can or has spoken the in the tongue of angels, he is setting an impossibly high standard, in order to demonstrate his point.

	SOLITUIDE CHART	
Pre-Event	**Solitude**	**Post-Events**
Matthew 14:13; John the Baptist beheaded by Herod	Jesus withdrew to a lonely place alone.	The multitude followed
Matthew 14:23; Feeding of the 5,000	Went up to the mountain alone, to pray.	Was still there when night fell.
Mt 26:36-46; Jesus soul was deeply grieved.	Jesus went into the garden Of Gethsemane to pray. He took his men with him, but he went into the garden alone. Three times he returned to his men, but each time he returned to the garden to pray more.	Jesus was ready to face the ordeal of his trial.
Mark 1:35; In previous passages, Jesus has healed many, and cast out demons, who recognized him for who he was.	Jesus arose early in the morning, and sought solitude to pray.	Jesus was ready to preach in the nearby towns.
The 5000 were feed, and the multitudes were taught.	Jesus went to the mountainside to pray.	Jesus went to the disciples By walking on the water.
Mark 7:24; Jesus traveled to a new region, Tyre.	Jesus was seeking solitude, but Was unable to find it.	Jesus healed the daughter of the Syrophoenician women of the demon.
Luke 6:12-13; Once again, Jesus has sought solitude on a mountainside.	In preparation for choosing his disciples, Jesus went to the Mountainside, and spent the whole night in prayer.	Jesus knew who he was to call, and he choose 12 to be apostles.
John 6:14-15; The 5000 have been fed, and the people recognize Jesus as a great prophet.	Jesus recognizes that his ministry is in danger, because the multitude Would force him to become King.	The lord sought solitude on the mountain.

Table 4. Prayer/Solitude chart from the Gospels

The Christian Life

One topic that needs to accompany any discussion of Pneumatology is how one should live after regeneration. We know that the Holy Spirit indwells us, that is, that the Spirit lives within us, to assist us in walking in a Christ-like fashion. There are several books in the New Testament that speak to believers about this issue. James, and 1 Peter are the two that most readily come to mind. So it is immediately obvious that, in order to live as a Christian, one must stay within the word of God. One must study to show oneself approved, so to speak. And, after a careful study of Bible, one comes to the conclusion that, while we are saved by grace, that we are compelled by that self-same grace to obey the commands of Christ. We must live as a people set apart, as examples to the unbelieving world. But the issue goes much deeper than simple obedience. Children know that they should obey their parents, and yet they still disobey. What is it about Christianity that makes it possible for a believer to live for Christ?

One aspect that comes immediately to mind is prayer. A Christian is only as strong as his or her prayer life. And where can one turn for an example of an active prayer life? To our savior, Jesus Christ. Table 4 shows some examples from the gospels in which Jesus sought out solitude, and conversed with the Father. If Jesus needed prayer to help sustain Him, then it follows that believers today would do well to follow His example. Another area that is all too often ignored are the lives of spiritual leaders from the Bible. What better way to learn to model spiritual leadership, and Christ-like behavior, than from men who have gone before, and whose stories are forever preserved in the word of God? For a study of one such man, the apostle Paul, see Appendix A. With the assistance of the Holy Spirit, Paul spread the Gospel throughout the known world of his day, and in so doing, allowed it to be spread throughout the entire world of our day.

Angelology
Chapter Six

General characteristics

God created innumerable hosts of spirit being called angels. The angels were created with personality, moral purity, moral freedom and immortality. The following is found in scriptures about angels:

1. They are spirit beings.

   > [13]But to which of the angels has He ever said, "SIT AT MY RIGHT HAND, UNTIL I MAKE YOUR ENEMIES A FOOTSTOOL FOR YOUR FEET"? [14]Are they not all ministering spirits, sent out to render service for the sake of those who will inherit salvation?
   > - Hebrews 1:13-14

2. They are created beings. In addition to the verse presented below, see Nehemiah 9:6; and Colossians 1:16.

> ²Praise Him, all His angels; Praise Him, all His hosts! ³Praise Him, sun and moon; Praise Him, all stars of light! ⁴Praise Him, highest heavens, And the waters that are above the heavens! ⁵ Let them praise the name of the LORD, For He commanded and they were created.
> - Psalms 148:2-5

3. They are innumerable. In addition to the verse presented below, see Daniel 7:10 and Hebrews 12:1.

> ¹¹Then I looked, and I heard the voice of many angels around the throne and the living creatures and the elders; and the number of them was myriad's of myriad's, and thousands of thousands,
> - Revelations 5:11

4. They have a personality. For a demonstration of this attribute, see 2 Samuel 14:20; Luke 1:19, 26; and Revelation 22:8-9.

5. They were created without sin. Genesis 1:31 gives a general validation, in that it says that everything that God created was good. But Jude 6 is a more specific reference, albeit a negative one.

> ²¹God created the great sea monsters and every living creature that moves, with which the waters swarmed after their kind, and every winged bird after its kind; and God saw that it was good.
> - Genesis 1:31

> ^{6}And angels who did not keep their own domain, but abandoned their proper abode, He has kept in eternal bonds under darkness for the judgment of the great day,
>
> - Jude 6

6. They were created with moral freedom. See 2 Peter 2:4:

> ^{4}For if God did not spare angels when they sinned, but cast them into hell and committed them to pits of darkness, reserved for judgment;

7. They are immortal.

> ^{6}for they cannot even die anymore, because they are like angels, and are sons of God, being sons of the resurrection.
>
> - Luke 20:36

Satan and the Fallen Angels

Satan was formerly one of God's holy angels[23] called Lucifer, and committed the first sin in the universe by a willful act of rebellion. This made him the father of lies and iniquity and as a result, led a great number of angels to follow in his sin.
These evil angels were confirmed in unrighteousness, some are chained into everlasting judgment, while some are free to move around and carry out the work of Satan under the permissive will of God. Listed below are some characteristics of Satan and his minions.

1. Satan is the chief adversary. In addition to the scripture presented below, see Job 1:9, 11-12; Zechariah 3:1; and revelation 12:10 for a demonstration of this characteristic.

---

[23] Technically, Satan was a Cherub, not an Angel. See Ezekiel 28:14.

> [6]"Now there was a day when the sons of God came to present themselves before the LORD, and Satan also came among them.
>
> - Job 1:6

2. Satan was of the highest rank before his sin.

   > [14]"You were the anointed cherub who covers, And I placed you *there*. You were on the holy mountain of God; You walked in the midst of the stones of fire.
   >
   > - Ezekiel 28:14

   > [12]"How you have fallen from heaven, O star of the morning, son of the dawn! You have been cut down to the earth, You who have weakened the nations! [13]But you said in your heart, 'I will ascend to heaven; I will raise my throne above the stars of God, And I will sit on the mount of assembly In the recesses of the north.[14]I will ascend above the heights of the clouds; I will make myself like the Most High.'
   >
   > - Isaiah 14:12-14

2. Satan fell from Grace. The following scriptures illustrate Satan's fall. Ezekiel 28:12-15 and Isaiah 14:1-14

3. Satan is the moral father of iniquity. In Addition to the scripture presented, John 8:44, see Matthew 13:36-39 for a demonstration of this characteristic.

   > [44]"You are of *your* father the devil, and you want to do the desires of your father. He was a murderer from the beginning, and does not stand in the truth because there is no truth in him.

> Whenever he speaks a lie, he speaks from his own *nature,* for he is a liar and the father of lies.

4. The fallen angels are confirmed in their unrighteousness. Some have already been chained in Tartarus. See 2 Peter 2:4 and Jude 6.

5. Others are still free to work against believers and the world. In addition to 1 Kings 22:22; see Job 1:6-12; Matthew 4:1-11; and Mark 5:2.

   > [22]"The LORD said to him, 'How?' And he said, 'I will go out and be a deceiving spirit in the mouth of all his prophets.' Then He said, 'You are to entice *him* and also prevail. Go and do so.'
   >
   > - 1 King's 22:22

6. They serve Satan.

   > [2]in which you formerly walked according to the course of this world, according to the prince of the power of the air, of the spirit that is now working in the sons of disobedience.
   >
   > - Ephesians 2:2

   > [11]Put on the full armor of God, so that you will be able to stand firm against the schemes of the devil. [12]For our struggle is not against flesh and blood, but against the rulers, against the powers, against the world forces of this darkness, against the spiritual *forces* of wickedness in the heavenly *places.*
   >
   > - Ephesians 6:11-12

7. The final destiny of these angels is the Lake of Fire. In addition to Matthew 25:41, which follows, see Jude 6; and Revelation 20:10 for a demonstration.

> ⁴¹"Then He will also say to those on His left, 'Depart from Me, accursed ones, into the eternal fire which has been prepared for the devil and his angels;
>
> - Matthew 25:41

8. Believers can and should resist his power

   > ⁷Submit therefore to God. Resist the devil and he will flee from you.
   >
   > - James 4:7

9. Satan is a defeated enemy and is no match for a spirit filled believer

   > ¹⁴Therefore, since the children share in flesh and blood, He Himself likewise also partook of the same, that through death He might render powerless him who had the power of death, that is, the devil,
   >
   > - Hebrews 2:14

   > ⁴You are from God, little children, and have overcome them; because greater is He who is in you than he who is in the world.
   >
   > - 1 John 4:4

The Angelic servants of the Most High

The holy angels who did not follow Lucifer, but kept their first estate are confirmed in holiness and are ministering spirits sent by God to minister to nations, to individual believers, and to God.

1. They are confirmed in righteousness. In addition to the scripture presented, see 1 Timothy 5:21

> [10]"See that you do not despise one of these little ones, for I say to you that their angels in heaven continually see the face of My Father who is in heaven.
>
> - Matthew 18:10

2. They are sent by God. See Psalms 103:20-21; and Daniel 10:10-15.

3. They minister in the affairs of the nations.

   > [12]Then he said to me, "Do not be afraid, Daniel, for from the first day that you set your heart on understanding *this* and on humbling yourself before your God, your words were heard, and I have come in response to your words. [13]"But the prince of the kingdom of Persia was withstanding me for twenty-one days; then behold, Michael, one of the chief princes, came to help me, for I had been left there with the kings of Persia.
   >
   > - Daniel 10:12-13

4. They minister to believers.

   > [14]Are they not all ministering spirits, sent out to render service for the sake of those who will inherit salvation?
   >
   > - Hebrews 1:14

   > [19]But during the night an angel of the Lord opened the gates of the prison, and taking them out he said,
   >
   > - Acts 5:19

5. They minister to God.

> [7]and *to give* relief to you who are afflicted and to us as well when the Lord Jesus will be revealed from heaven with His mighty angels in flaming fire,
> - 2 Thessalonians 1:7

It is important to note that angels are created beings. They are mentioned often in scripture, but only three are named. These three are Satan, Michael, and Gabriel.

TEACHINGS OF THE COLOSSIAN HERESY

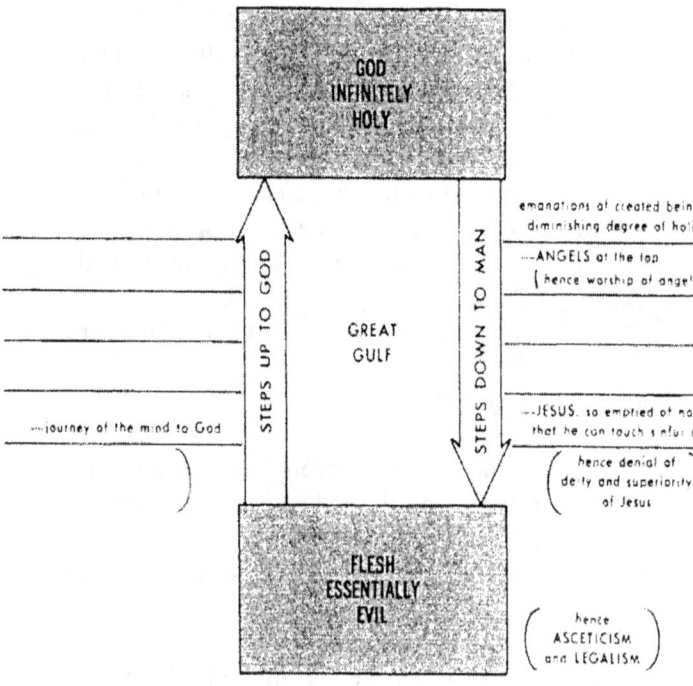

Table 5. Jensen's Teachings of the Colossian Heresies

Of the fallen angels, only Satan is named. In appearance, angels always appear as men. That is, they never appear with wings. That is not to say that there are no angels who are winged. The cherubim are described as winged. It is equally important to note that angels, as created beings, are not worthy of worship. There was a heretical problem among the early church with Gnostics who placed Jesus on a level below the angels, because he had been human. Paul addressed this in the book of Colossians. Table 5 is a chart taken from *Jensen's Survey of the New Testament*[24], which Dr. Jensen explains the chart in the following manner:

> The chart "teachings of the Colossian Heresy" shows what were probably the bases for the speculative doctrines of the Colossian heresy. The false religionists attempted to solve the problem of the great gulf. What was that problem? Two solutions have been suggested.
>
> 1. God reaching man by way of emanations from Himself, each successive emanation being of less holiness. Jesus is regarded as being less holy than the angels.
>
> 2. Man reaching God in the realm of mental activity.
>
> Since flesh was regarded as essentially evil, asceticism and legalism were the consequences.

[24] Jensen, Irving. Jensen's Survey of the New Testament. 342-343

Anthropology
Chapter Seven

Essential elements

God formed man form the dust of the earth. Man was created in God's image and was called Adam. Man possessed an original righteousness and a moral nature that had not been tested in a choice of good or evil. Adam constituted the entire human race in his power of choice between good and evil.

1. Man was created from the dust Genesis 2:7 illustrates this well.

2. He was made in God's image.

    [26]Then God said, "Let Us make man in Our image, according to Our likeness; and let them

> rule over the fish of the sea and over the birds of the sky and over the cattle and over all the earth, and over every creeping thing that creeps on the earth." ²⁷God created man in His own image, in the image of God He created him; male and female He created them.
>
> - Genesis 1:26-27

3. He was made perfect in holiness. Genesis 1:31 teaches that all things created by God were Good. This applies to man as well as to the angels. See also Ecclesiastes 7:29; and genesis 1:27.

4. Adam constituted the entire human race.

   > ¹²Therefore, just as through one man sin entered into the world, and death through sin, and so death spread to all men, because all sinned—
   >
   > - Romans 5:12

   > ¹⁹For as through the one man's disobedience the many were made sinners, even so through the obedience of the One the many will be made righteous.
   >
   > - Romans 5:19

The test

God made Eve to be the helpmeet to the man. While still in their condition of innocence, they were subjected to a moral test, which they failed because of the influence of Satan. Their failure was the introduction of sin into the human race. See 1 Timothy 2:13-14 for evidence of this.

> ¹³For it was Adam who was first created, *and* then Eve. ¹⁴And *it was* not Adam *who* was

deceived, but the woman being deceived, fell into transgression.

1. Eve was created to be a helpmate. See Genesis 2:18-23 for the story of Eve's creation.

2. Adam and Eve were subjects of a moral test. See Genesis 2:16-27 for a description.

3. Adam and Eve failed that test. Genesis 3:1-19 tells the entire story, but 1 Timothy 2:13-14 gives some insight into the scenario.

4. Their failure brought sin and death into the race. See Romans 5:12.

Sin and its effect on mankind

Sin is the failure to conform to the moral law God in act, disposition or state. Sin is the result of a moral creature's choice of self as the chief object of affection. It is also a positional truth in that all mankind has missed the mark of righteousness before God.

1. Sin is non-conformity to God's law in act;

> [23]for all have sinned and fall short of the glory of God,
> - Romans 3:23

2. In disposition:

> [7]because the mind set on the flesh is hostile toward God; for it does not subject itself to the law of God, for it is not even able *to do so*,
> - Romans 8:7

3. Or in state.

> [5]Behold, I was brought forth in iniquity, And in sin my mother conceived me.
> - Psalms 51:5

> [5]even when we were dead in our transgressions, made us alive together with Christ (by grace you have been saved),
> - Ephesians 2:5

> [4]Everyone who practices sin also practices lawlessness; and sin is lawlessness.
> -1 John 3:4

4. Sin results from the exaltation of self above God. Again Genesis gives the example from Scripture. See Chapter 3, verses 1-6.

The consequence of Adam's sin included immediate spiritual death resulting in the cessation of fellowship with God. It resulted in subsequent physical death in the separation of soul and body. It gave man a depraved nature in the loss of all ability to choose God over self without divine assistance. The end result of sin is death and a sentence of eternal punishment in the Lake of Fire. All men suffer the consequences of Adam's sin by virtue of their presence in Adam.

How the study of creation science affects Anthropology

As a creationist, this author rejects the idea of evolution. Creation scientists have gathered evidence that gives much credence to the position that man was created much as he exists today. But that brings up the question, "Why did men have such dramatically long life spans before the Flood?"

> And God said, This is the token of the covenant which I make between me and you and every living creature that is with you, for perpetual generations: I do set my bow in the cloud, and it shall be for a token of a covenant between me and the earth.
> - *Genesis 9:12-13 King James Version*

> A man came to a Rabbi and asked him this question: "Why did the early generations live so long?" The Rabbi replied: "Adam lived nearly a thousand years because God told him that he would die on the day of his sin, and God's day lasts a thousand years. If his son Seth had not lived almost as long, Adam would have had no one to take care of him during his declining years, for a grandson usually does not feel bound to support a grandfather. And so it was until Noah came. He was willing to support all his forefathers alive in his time. Therefore, after the flood, the years of men diminished."[25]

The account above was taken from *The Talmudic Anthology: Tales and Teachings of the Rabbis*, edited by Louis I. Newman, in collaboration with Samuel Spitz. While it certainly is an interesting account, this author cannot help but take exception to it in several places. The first problem that is about the length of God's days. Henry Morris and John Whitcomb state that:

> "since God's revealed word describes this creation as taking place in six "days" and since there apparently is no contextual basis for understanding these days in any sort of symbolic

---

[25] Tanna de-Be Eliyahu Rabbah, 16

> sense, it is an act of both faith and reason to accept them, literally, as real days."[26]

The law of sufficient reason also bears this out. This hermeneutical principle, formulated by Gottfried Von Leibnitz in the mid 1600s states that one must not jump to conclusions, but base conclusions on adequate grounds. This law teaches that we must review the usage of a word, words, or a doctrine as it is used throughout scripture, and to understand it thoroughly before drawing a conclusion. In this case, if one carefully studies the uses of the word "days"; as in days of creation, one can not help but come to the conclusion that the author is referring to literal, twenty-four hour days. It is true, that in Psalm 90:4 the scripture says *For a thousand years in thy sight are like yesterday when it passes by*, but this is clearly figurative language, or better yet, a poetic expression which is being used by Moses to express the awesome majesty of God. This scripture is also quoted by peter in 2 peter 3:8, but Rab Eliyahu would hardly quote from that source, even if it was available to him! In Marvin Lubenow's *Bones of Contention* Chapter 20, old earth-old Adam Creationist Davis Young is quoted from a lecture given at Wheaton college in 1990:

> The Day-Age hypothesis insisted with at least a semblance of textual plausibility that the days of creation were long periods of time of indeterminate length, although the immediate context implies that the term *yom* for "day" really means "day". Having devised a means for allowing Genesis 1 to be in harmony with an ancient planet, Day-Age advocates needed to demonstrate that the sequence of creative activities of Genesis chapter 1 matched the sequence of events deciphered by the astronomers and geologists. Well, Day-Agers outdid themselves in constructing impressive

---

[26] Whitcomb and Morris, *The Genesis Flood;* p. 228

correlations. Of course, these correlations...all differed from each other. While a fairly convincing case could be made for a general concord,...specifics of these correlations were a bit murky.

There were some textual obstacles the Day-Agers developed an amazing agility in surmounting. The Biblical text, for example, has vegetation appearing on the third day and animals on the fifth day. Geology, however, has long realized that invertebrate animals were swarming in the seas long before vegetation gained a foothold on the land. This obvious point of conflict, however, failed to dissuade well-intentioned Christians, my earlier self included, from nudging the text to mean something different from what it says. In my case, I suggested that the events of the days overlapped. Having publicly repented of that textual mutilation a few years ago, I will move on without further embarrassing myself.

Worse yet, the text states that on the fourth day God made the heavenly bodies after the earth was already in existence. Here is a blatant naked confrontation with science. Astronomy insists that the sun is older than the earth. How do Day-Agers worm out of this? The usual subterfuge involves the suggestion that the light originally visible on earth was sunlight that was obscured and diffused by the thick atmospheric mists that began to dissipate with the separation of the waters on the second day. Not until the fourth day, then, had the mists thinned to the point where the sun became visible from the earth.[27]

---

[27] "The Harmonization of Scripture and Science," A Symposium held at Wheaton College, March 23, 1990.

The second problem that this Rabbinical "Teaching" presents for me is the reasons presented for the extraordinary ages attained by the pre-flood patriarchs. During the middle ages, when this tale was recorded, it was customary for a son to care for his aged parents. This was a culturally diverse custom, practiced among many peoples, not just among the Jews. Indeed, this was the primary motivating factor in the Asian peoples desire for Son's, rather than daughters.. A more plausible explanation is offered by Morris and Whitcomb, taken once again from THE definitive work on flood geology, *The Genesis Flood.*[28]

> And, incidentally, the declining life span after the flood seems to fit in perfectly with our concept of the dissipation of the earth's protective blanket during the flood. As we have noted, this canopy of water vapor (with probably also large amounts of Carbon Dioxide and ozone augmenting the effect) provided a warm, pleasant, presumably healthful environment throughout the world. Perhaps the most important effect of the canopy was a shielding action provided against the intense radiations impinging upon the earth from space. Short wave-length radiation, as well as the bombardment of elementary particles of all kinds, is known to have damaging effects-both somatic and genetic effects-on organisms and this is generally true for all types of radiations.
>
> With respect to somatic (non-hereditary) effects, research is only very recently bringing to light some of the damage that can be done by radiation. It is now common knowledge, of course, that large doses of radiation can be fatal, and this is one of the most feared aspects of

---

[28] Whitcomb and Morris, Pages 399-401.

possible nuclear warfare. But even small amounts, if long continued, may well be very harmful. Cancer and leukemia, among others, are possibilities that are being seriously studied.

Statistical studies on life-spans as affected by radiation intensities are very pertinent to our present discussion. Austin Brues, Director of the Biological and Medical Research Division of the Argonne National laboratory, says:

> Such experiments have shown that a single dose of radiation which does not kill an animal within the period of acute radiation sickness may tend to shorten life...Studies using radiation may lead to an understanding of this most universal, but least understood, fact about life, the aging process.[29]

Dr. Shields Warren, a specialist in cancer research, also writes in this vein:

> There is much evidence that overdoses of radiation lead to premature aging. Both animal experiments and observations of the life spans of radiologists indicate that a dose of 1000 roentgens received over a long period of time may well shorten the life span about 10 percent. Data on the longevity of more than 82,000 physicians indicate that the average length of life of those not known to have had contact with radiation in the period of 1930 through 1954

---

[29] Austin M. Brues: "Somatic Effects of Radiation, "Bulletin of the Atomic Scientists, Vol. 14, January 1958, pp. 13-14

> was 65.7 years as against an average life span of 60.5 years for the radiologists. Not only is leukemia more prevalent among those exposed, but death from causes such as heart disease and arteriosclerosis also appears to come at an earlier age. In fact, radiologists succumbed at an earlier age to practically every type of disease, indicating that the damage done to the body is widespread in its influence.[30]

Similarly, George Beadle, Nobel laureate for his work in biochemical genetics and head of the Biology Department at California Institute of Technology, writes:

> In experimental animals, the mouse for example, sublethal doses of radiation appreciably reduce the life span. It is almost certain that this also occurs in man. Most investigators agree that there is no threshold below which ionizing radiation has no effect on living matter.[31] If such effects can be observed in a short life time as a result of artificial radiations, it is certainly possible that much greater effects on longevity would have been produced over the millenniums by natural background radiation.

On pages 404-405 of *The Genesis Flood*, authors Whitcomb and Morris wrap up this particular discussion as follows:

> But to return to the question of antediluvian longevity, it surely is quite reasonable in view of what is known about the somatic and genetic

---

[30] Shields, Warren: "Radiation and the Human Body," Scientific Monthly, Vol. 84, January 1957, p. 5.
[31] George W. Beadle: "Ionizing Radiation and the Citizen," Scientific American, Vol. 201, September 1959, p. 224.

effects of radiations to infer that, over the centuries since the flood, the accumulation of these effects in man in particular has resulted in gradual deterioration and decreasing life-span.[32] Especially marked must have been the effect in the centuries *immediately* after the Flood, in view of the precipitation of the earth's vapor blanket, which previously had filtered out practically all the environmental radiation which is now found in our troposphere. Little has been done as yet on the subject of the effect of these "natural" radiations, but such information as is available clearly indicates that their effect is similar to that of artificial radiations. It is quite possible that most spontaneous mutations are ultimately attributable to the natural radiation in the environment; that is, the sun's ultra-violet rays, cosmic radiation products, radiocarbon, etc. The committee concurs that these spontaneous mutations are also harmful:

Like radiation-induced mutations, nearly all spontaneous mutations with detectable effects are harmful.

Before the Flood, therefore, everything was conducive to physical health and longevity. Equable temperatures, freedom from environmental radiation's, and other factors attributable to the vapor canopy all contributed to this effect. Nevertheless, sin and death and the curse were also realities then as much as now.

---

[32] Other suggested causes for declining longevity are changes in diet and inbreeding. See Arthur Custance: Longevity in Antiquity. Doorway Papers, No. 2, Privately printed, Ottawa, 1957.

After the Flood, the canopy was precipitated, its protective effects largely removed, and then began a long decline in general health and longevity, only partly offset in recent decades by advances in medicine and public health engineering. Much of this decline, as well as other effects we have already discussed, can undoubtedly be attributed to the greatly increased incidence of radiation upon the earth's surface and upon its inhabitants. Probably during and immediately after the Flood this increase was very sharp; the present equilibrium was gradually established by the inauguration of the present hydrologic cycle.

The author's experience and education concerning Nuclear Power tends to lend credence to the theory presented by Whitcomb and Morris with regard to the protection from cosmic and ultra-violet radiation by a pre-Flood vapor Canopy. It is well known that three things will help reduce
dosages of Ionizing radiation. Time; Distance; and Shielding. Time means to limit your exposure to the minimum amount of time necessary to accomplish whatever task you are performing. Distance means to put as much distance between yourself and the source as possible, and shielding is the subject of interest to our topic.

The two best types of shielding are lead, and water. The area between the Reactor compartment and the Operations compartment on U. S. Navy submarines has a lead lining. The Reactor Vessel itself is surrounded by both primary and
secondary shielding, which are water tanks and a system of piping. The lead serves to prevent radiation from leaking past. Water serves as follows; it dissipates heat, and also prevents radiation leakage. Isn't it interesting that in the thousands of

years between earth's creation, and the invention of the Nuclear Submarine, that nothing better than God's own original buffer could be found or invented?

Another interesting point is in the life span of certain fishes. Carps and certain varieties of Goldfish, to be specific. Scientists have no real way of knowing how old they can life to be, but it appears that they can live to a very old age. Nor do scientists really understand why. I know that it is mere supposition to suggest that it could be that the water helps shield UV radiation, because then why don't all fish age more slowly, or for that matter, why not humans who spend lots of time under water?

This author would like to go on record, that as to George Beadle's observation that in addition to reducing their lifespan, introducing sublethal dosages of ionizing radiation to laboratory mice also greatly irritates them and makes them generally cranky!

Archaeology and Anthropology

Some may ask, "Why is the study of Archaeology important when studying the biblical doctrine of man?" The answer is that it offers hard, conclusive evidence about the origin of man, as well as physical evidence in support of biblical events. However, just as questionable scriptures should never be used to support biblical doctrines, questionable archaeological practices should also be avoided. In his book *The Bible as History*, Werner Keller purports to attempt to "prove" the bible through archacological and historical means. What he really is doing, or trying to do, is disprove. In the chapter "Digging up the Flood", we follow the excavation of Ur by the famous Archaeologist Sir Charles Leonard Woolley. During his excavations, he discovers "proof" of Noah's flood. But judge for yourself whether Keller offers proof of Noah's flood as documented in scripture...

When after several days some of Woolley's workman called out to him "we are on ground level" he let himself down on the floor of the shaft to satisfy himself. Traces of any kind of settlement did in fact abruptly break off in the shaft. The last fragments of household utensils lay on the smooth flat surface of the base of the pit. Here and there were charred remains. Woolley's first thought was: "This is it at last." He carefully prodded the ground on the floor of the shaft and stopped short: it was clay, pure clay of a kind that could only be deposited by water! Clay in a place like that? Woolley tried to find an explanation: it must be the accumulated silt of the Euphrates in bygone days. This stratum must have come into existence when the great river thrust its delta far out of the sea at the river mouth at the rate of 75 feet a year. When Ur was in its heyday, the Euphrates flowed so close to it that the great staged tower was reflected in it's waters and the Gulf was visible from the temple on its summit. The first buildings must therefore have sprung up on the mud flats of the delta.

Measurements of the adjacent area and more careful calculations brought Woolley eventually however to a different conclusion. "I saw that we were much too high up. It was most unlikely that the island on which the first settlement was built stood up so far out of the marsh."

The foot of the shaft, where the layer of clay began, was several yards above the foot of the river level. It could not therefore be river deposit. What was the meaning then of this remarkable stratum? Where did it come from? None of his associates could give him a satisfactory answer. They decided to dig on and make the shaft deeper. Woolley gazed intently as once more basket after basket came out of the trench and their contents were examined. Deeper and deeper went the spades into the ground, 3 feet, 6 feet-still pure clay. Suddenly at nearly 10 feet the layer of clay stopped as abruptly as it had started. What would come now?

The next baskets that came to the surface gave an answer that none of the expedition would have dreamt of. They could hardly believe their eyes. They had expected virgin soil. But what emerged into the glaring sunshine was rubble and more rubble, ancient rubbish and countless potsherds. Under this clay deposit almost ten feet thick they had struck fresh evidence of human habitation. The appearance and quality of the pottery had noticeably altered. Above the clay-stratum were jars and bowls that had obviously been turned on the potter's wheel,

Here on the contrary, they were hand-made. No matter how carefully they sifted the contents of the baskets, amid increasing excitement, metal remains were nowhere to be found, the primitive implement that did emerge was made of hewn flint. It must belong to the stone age!

That day a telegram from Mesopotamia flashed what was perhaps the most extraordinary message that had ever stirred men's imaginations "We have found the flood". The incredible discovery at Ur made headline news in the United States and Britain.

The Flood-that was the only possible explanation of this great clay deposit beneath the hill at Ur, which quite clearly separated two epochs of settlement. The sea had left its unmistakable traces in the shape of remains of little marine organisms embedded in the clay. Woolley had to confirm his conclusions without delay: a chance coincidence-although the odds were against it-might conceivably have been making fools of them. Three hundred yards from the first shaft he sank a second one.

The spades produced the same result: sherds-clay-fragments of hand-made pottery.

Finally to remove all doubt, Woolley made them dig a shaft through the rubble where the old settlement lay on a natural hill, that is to say, on a considerably higher level than the stratum of clay.

Just at about the same level as in the two other shafts the sherds of wheel-turned vessels stopped suddenly. Immediately beneath them came hand-made clay pots. It was exactly as Woolley had supposed and expected. Naturally the intermediate layer of clay was missing. "About sixteen feet below a brick pavement," noted Woolley, "Which we could with reasonable Certainty date about 2700 B.C. we were among the ruins of that Ur which had existed before the Flood."

How far down did the layer of clay extend? What area was affected by the disaster? A proper hunt now started for traces of the flood in other parts of Mesopotamia. Other archaeologists discovered a further important check-point near Kish, south-east of Babylon, where the Euphrates and the Tigris flow in a great bend towards each other. There they found a similar band of clay, but only 18 inches thick. Gradually by a variety of tests the limits of the Flood waters could be established. According to

Woolley the disaster engulfed an area northwest of the Persian Gulf amounting to 400 miles long and 100 miles wide, looking at the map we should call it "a local occurrence"-for the inhabitants of the river plains it was however in those days their whole world.

After endless enquiry and attempts at some explanation, without achieving any concrete results, any hope of solving the great riddle of the flood had long since been given up. It seemed to lie in a dark and distant region of time which we could never hope to penetrate. Now Woolley and his associates had through their tireless and patient efforts made a discovery which shattered even the experts: a vast catastrophic inundation, resembling the Biblical Flood which had regularly been described by sceptics as either a fairy tale or a legend, had not only taken place but was moreover an event within the compass of history.

At the foot of the old staged tower of the Sumerians, at Ur on the lower Euphrates, anyone could climb down a ladder into a narrow shaft and see and touch the remains of a gigantic and catastrophic Flood which had deposited a layer of clay almost 10 feet thick. Reckoning by the age of the strata containing traces of human habitation, and in this respect they are as reliable as a calendar, it could also be ascertained when the great Flood took place. It happened about 4000 B.C..

Clearly people in Woolley's day tended to give dramatic interpretations to the results of excavations more readily than they do nowadays, for shortly after Woolley, another excavator, Stephen Langdon, claimed, "with strong support from the press", that he in turn had found, in Kish, that is to say, in Babylon, "material traces of the Flood". It was Langdon's, but also Woolley's bad luck that the datings of these two flood catastrophes did not agree. Which flood was the right one, the genuine, Biblical Flood? Woolley protested vigorously against Langdon's claim to have discovered it and a vehement argument followed which, however, did not in the least disturb a number of writers, among them, for example, Sir Charles Marston, who asserted that both Wooley and Langdon had discovered "simultaneously the deposits left by the Flood".

Since then the excitement has somewhat subsided and given place to more sober consideration. The following four main points emerge from the pronouncements of the experts:-

Of Woolley's five shafts only two revealed any deposits at all from an inundation.

The inundation at Ur did not lead to the abandonment of the settlement. In fact, it did not even lead to an interruption in occupation.

Traces of inundation were indeed discovered in other places in Mesopotamia, in Kish, as well as in Fara (Shuruppak), Ninevah and Uruk (Erech) but on the other hand, they are not found where they ought to be present if the whole of Mesopotamia was flooded.

The traces left by the inundations at the various excavation sites also vary, in some cases quite appreciably, in their chronological sequence. They belong to quite different periods; centuries separate them.

In other words, Woolley's "Flood" was obviously not of sufficient magnitude for the

Biblical "Flood", unless we assume that one of the flood catastrophes shown by archaeology to have occurred in Mesopotamia had nevertheless had such a lasting effect on the inhabitants of those days that-with a considerable amount of exaggeration-the tradition of a catastrophe to humanity could arise from it. Naturally, however, this is mere supposition and the Biblical Flood, at any rate, a flood of unimaginable extent described in the Bible, still remains "archaeologically not demonstrated". The question consequently remains; do all the various "flood" reports, which occur in practically all parts of the world, describe merely mankind's earliest experience of the phenomenon "flood catastrophe" and were all the traditional, relevant accounts of floods simply compressed or exaggerated to form a number of stories of the "great flood of all floods" or are they the vestiges of much older traditions going back hundreds of years *before* Woolley's Flood at Ur, to the time of the melting of the Gigantic glaciers of the Ice Age when the ocean rose some two hundred meters and the limits of today's land and sea were formed? That event had world-wide consequences which could explain why the traditions of a flood have persisted among so many peoples.

The rebuttal will begin with the fact that Woolley (and Keller) are so very surprised to discover a layer of clay. Evidence of a world-wide flood can be found virtually everywhere! On top of the highest mountains fossil trilobites are routinely discovered. So the fact that a layer of silt was discovered should come as no extraordinary shock.

The next blunder (which was eventually caught by the unidentified "experts") was the fact that on both sides of the strata are evidence of habitation. Come on now. After 371 days of the flood, this author is certain that Noah did not head straight to the site where Ur had previously existed, and build on the same site. How could he have known the exact location? Not to mention that people stayed in the general area of Babylon until dispersed. additionally how much time does Mr. Keller feel elapsed between the strata? He seems to indicate that because there was a difference in the quality of the pottery that mankind passed from the stone age directly to metals directly after the flood! That's pretty fast progress! Of course, the difference in the quality of pottery and the presence of metal type tools does indicate significant progress, but why does Mr. Keller suppose that pre-flood humans had no metal crafting capabilities? The thought process of Mr. Keller clearly indicates that he has found what he believed that he would find. He had presupposed that pre-flood man was primitive, and so he searched for archaeological evidence that would indeed support his hypothesis, and of course he found it. This circular thought process is extremely common among evolutionists. To help make my point, let me again quote from Dr. Lubenow's *Bones of Contention,* this time from chapter 2, "An Inexact Kind of Science":

> The flaw is known in logic as begging the question. In begging the question, you assume the thing to be true the very thing you are trying to prove. Let me illustrate.
>
> A man in Chicago was observed walking down the street snapping his fingers. Finally, someone was driven by curiosity to ask him why he repeatedly snapped his fingers. "It keeps the elephants away," the man replied. "why, man, there aren't any elephants within ten thousand miles of this place!" Responded his questioner. "Pretty effective, isn't it?"

exclaimed the man. The first man assumed that his finger snapping kept the elephants away. He then used the absence of elephants to prove the effectiveness of his actions. To presuppose the truth of what you are trying to prove is the illogical practice of begging the question.

Another problem with Mr. Keller's account of Woolley's excavation of Ur is in the shafts, or rather in the digging of them. Imagine the amount of time it must have taken to dig this enormous shaft. Now add the time required to dig two more shafts. Remember that bearers, rather than machinery, or a large drill, were used, not only to dig each of the shafts, but to remove the dirt, sludge, and debris. Yet Mr. Keller would have you believe that this was a quick process. Whether that is to deceive, or rather, to keep up the suspense of the story, I do not know. I do know that the excavation of Ur took many seasons, and it was by no means a rapid process.

The problem with Mr. Keller's book, and not just the chapter on the "flood", is that it is bad archaeology. Werner Keller was a scholar, but he was not widely traveled. Nor was he known for his field work. But that did not stop him from writing this highly acclaimed, often quoted book. I guess if you make it sound scholarly enough, people will believe it is.

The last problem with this particular chapter is from the last paragraph quoted, about the prevalence of flood traditions. It has been widely documented that flood traditions span the globe. Dr. Tim Lahaye, in his gripping book *The Ark on Ararat*, says the following:

> The remarkable similarity of all these traditions is evident. And even their differences appear in a predictable pattern, predictable, that is, if you assume that all are descendants of Noah and migrated from Ararat after the Flood.

As might be suspected local geography is usually specified when any is mentioned. The tribes "relocated" their landing place to the nearest high mountain in most cases, making the personal impact of the story greater. The farther from the Mesopotamian area a tribe had migrated, the more incidental circumstances crept into the story, and the story in many cases took the viewpoint of an outside observer as opposed to Noah's seemingly confined observations. In fact, the references in the Bible to "the mountains of Ararat" is in itself important. The Israelites had no personal knowledge of the land to the north of Palestine before Moses' death. The reference to a specific mountain far from their land is quite unique. Some of the legends mention a faraway mountain, but never a specific one. Anthropologists feel that this testifies to the accuracy of the biblical account.

Animals consistently played a part. In many tales, birds or other animals were used directly to gauge or alter the recession of the flood waters during the latter stages. Frequently, animals were included in the Ark or were used to forewarn the survivors. In almost every case when a favored family or righteous ones were saved, they were forewarned. This would not necessarily be so if the traditions were unrelated, but the fact that there is a correlation verifies the biblical account.

In a few of the stories the striking and precise accounts of the appearance of the rainbow as a token after the flood, the sacrifice of thankfulness, and the specific mention of the salvation of an eight member family all appear. These details cannot be coincidental. They must stem from a common source. One would expect many traditions to incorporate the landing place of a mountain into their story, because in a time of severe flood, local or otherwise, a mountaintop or boat provides the most likely solution. But the other minute details are not what would be expected if the stories came from unrelated sources or events.

Critics of the global Flood theory have always been quick to claim that many of these Flood traditions actually come from contact with missionaries, reaching into out of the way places spreading the Christian faith. And, to be sure, one case of this has been documented in an Indian tribe in North America. But the use of that excuse must be rejected by a logical mind on several accounts. First, most of the traditions were gathered by those whose interests were purely anthropological, those whose motives did not include vindicating the Christian Bible, and any suspicion would be noted. In fact, many of the ancient written accounts, were penned by pagans who were very much in opposition to everything the Hebrews held dear.

Second, missionaries who dedicate their lives to spreading Christianity usually spend their time imparting the spiritual truths of the Gospel, not of Jewish history. If they felt a desire to relate the miraculous events of the past, we should find similar traditions of the miracles concerning Jonah and the whale, the crossing of the red Sea, the plagues of Egypt, destruction of Sodom and Gomorrah and others, equally worthy of incorporation into the body of folklore of a culture. But we find no such thing. We do find many, many traditions of the creation of the world, the fall of man into sin, and the Tower of Babel and confusion of tongues, but this is understandable. It was after these events that the nations began to disperse.

Third, if missionaries are responsible for the similarities in the stories, what, or who is responsible for the differences? Most of the stories tell of the Gods' disfavor with man. But the means of expressing such disfavor vary so widely that it cannot have come from a recent source wishing to convey meaningful truth. For instance, incurring the wrath of the almighty lizard man by irritating the river lizards corresponds to the Genesis account in concept, but such details could not have been passed along in recent times by anyone knowledgeable of the biblical story.

The conclusion must stand. The universal Flood traditions can only have come from a common source, embellished with local color and culture, but retaining enough pertinent data to convey both historical and moral concepts.

The evidence, when gathered, sufficiently refutes the attempt by Mr. Werner Keller to prove a local flood. But by no means is this concept confined to one rather obscure German scholar. This theory is probably the most widely held concept among those who wish to marry science with the Bible. Nor are all attempts as scholarly and well thought out as Mr. Keller's. The next account is possibly the most ridiculous attempt ever written. Once again I turn to Whitcomb and Morris's The Genesis Flood. Footnote 4 on pages 58 and 59 quote the following:

> To illustrate the extent to which some scholars will go in this direction, we quote from a paper read by Lt. Col. F. A. Molony, O.B.E., before the Victoria Institute in 1936: "Now the

part of the great Mesopotamian plain which lies below the 500' contour is as large as England without Wales. Hence it is probable that *Noah and his sons never saw a mountain in their lives*...Fifteen cubits is only about 23 feet, so it would seem that the word we translate "mountains" would be better rendered *mounds*, probably raised by human labor...The chronicler knew that the artificial mounds were very seldom more than 15 cubits high, so he wrote 'Fifteen cubits upward did the waters prevail; and the mountains were covered'." ("The Noachian Deluge and Its Probable Connection with Lake Van," *Journal of the Transactions of the Victoria Institute*, LXVIII [1936], pp. 44, 51, 52. Italics are ours.)

Col. Molony went on to explain that the Flood was caused by a sudden emptying of Lake Van (in eastern Turkey) into the Mesopotamian Valley. Lifting the Ark above the artificial mounds, the lake water threatened to sweep it out into the Persian Gulf. But in order to avoid such a fate, Noah "may have rigged jury masts and sails, and anchored when the wind was northerly." Comment hardly seems necessary!

Granted, this crackpot example is extreme in its ridiculousness. Bernard Ramm ascribes to a local Flood theory, and he is neither uneducated, nor ridiculous. He's wrong of course, but he never stoops to the level of the "Learned" Colonel Molony!

Hamartiology
Chapter Eight

The nature of God

The attributes of God have been discussed in some detail in previous chapters. In order to understand mans fallen state it is necessary to discuss some of these again, but perhaps from a different viewpoint.

God is Love. This is evidenced by such scriptures as John 3:16, and 1 John 4:8.

> [16]"For God so loved the world, that He gave His only begotten Son, that whoever believes in Him shall not perish, but have eternal life.
> - John 3:16

> [8]The one who does not love does not know God, for God is love.
>
> -1 John 4:8

Most people who are even slightly familiar with scripture know that God is Love. The liberal Churches focus almost exclusively upon this attribute. The problem is that it is only one of Gods attributes. The liberal Church asks the question "If God is so loving, why does He not just forgive us?" They believe that since God loves, that he will ultimately forgive all mankind.

The attribute that contrasts the most with God's love is God's Justness. The scripture that bests contrast these two attributes is Exodus 34:6-7.

> [6]Then the LORD passed by in front of him and proclaimed, "The LORD, the LORD God, compassionate and gracious, slow to anger, and abounding in lovingkindness and truth; [7]who keeps lovingkindness for thousands, who forgives iniquity, transgression and sin; yet He will by no means leave *the guilty* unpunished, visiting the iniquity of fathers on the children and on the grandchildren to the third and fourth generations."

It is because God is the sum of all of His attributes that it is necessary for Him to punish sin. He is Holy, and unable to tolerate sin.

The nature of Man

Man is prideful and foolish. He refuses to either accept the fact that he is sinful, or to acknowledge a God who will punish sin. Voltaire summed the problem up neatly: "God has created man in his own image, and man has been returning the favor ever since." The Bible teaches us about God's standards in the following scriptures:

> [10]as it is written, "THERE IS NONE RIGHTEOUS, NOT EVEN ONE; [11]THERE IS NONE WHO UNDERSTANDS, THERE IS NONE WHO SEEKS FOR GOD; [12]ALL HAVE TURNED ASIDE, TOGETHER THEY HAVE BECOME USELESS; THERE IS NONE WHO DOES GOOD, THERE IS NOT EVEN ONE."
> - Romans 3:10-12

> [10]For whoever keeps the whole law and yet stumbles in one *point,* he has become guilty of all.
> - James 2:10

We are all sinners. There has only been one man who was sinless, and we crucified Him.

The problem of sin

Dr. Charles Ryrie defines sin as follows:

> Sin is missing the mark, badness, rebellion, iniquity, going astray, wickedness, wandering, ungodliness, crime, lawlessness, transgression, ignorance, and a falling away.
> More briefly, sin has generally been defined as lawlessness. This is an accurate definition as long as law is conceived of in its broadest sense, that is, defection away from any of God's standards. Sin may also be defined as against the character of God.

Man has had a problem of sin since the Garden of Eden. Sin entered the world when Satan enticed Eve to taste of the fruit of the tree of knowledge. Since that time, anyone born of the seed of man from the womb of a woman has been tainted with this sin. In addition to the scriptures presented below, see the following scriptures for a demonstration of this principle: Psalm 38:3-4, 51:2-4; Isaiah 1:18; Matthew 26:28; Galatians 6:7-9; and 1 John 1:5-10, 2:1-2.

> [2]But your iniquities have made a separation between you and your God, And your sins have hidden *His* face from you so that He does not hear.
>
> - Isaiah 59:2

> [19]Now the deeds of the flesh are evident, which are: immorality, impurity, sensuality, [20]idolatry, sorcery, enmities, strife, jealousy, outbursts of anger, disputes, dissensions, factions, [21]envying, drunkenness, carousing, and things like these, of which I forewarn you, just as I have forewarned you, that those who practice such things will not inherit the kingdom of God.
>
> - Galatians 5:19-21

The solution for sin

Paul gives perhaps the most elegant answer to how to overcome man's sin problem in Romans 5:8-17. Sin has been described as a debt, a debt that must be paid. Sin has been described as a chasm that cannot be overcome with Jesus.

The difference between being temptation and trials

The best way to understand the concept of temptation is to study James 1:13-16.

> Let no one say when he is tempted, " I am being
> tempted by God"; for God cannot be tempted by
> evil, and He himself does not tempt anyone.
> - James 1:13

Who does the tempting? Not God, at any rate. God is sinless. God is blameless, God is perfect. He, by definition of His character, cannot be tempted. The word *tempted* used in this verse is different than the word used in verses 2 and 12. The word used in verses 2 and 12 is *Peirasmos*, meaning "those tests designed to try the quality of ones character". The word used here is *Peirazoo*, meaning a "solicitation to evil". One comes from God, and one from either the devil, or from our own fleshly desires, our own un-Godly appetites. Now examine Verse 14:

> But each one is tempted when he is carried away
> and enticed by his own lust.

So you can see that we are our own worst enemy! Our lusts lead to temptation......our wicked appetites are the snares by which we are captured. It is important to remember to whom James is speaking. He is writing to believers. Not for the benefit of the unsaved, but for the saints. If you don't believe that those who have been saved can stray, then explain why it would be necessary for these scriptures to be included within the Word of God.

This line of thinking can sometimes lead to the erroneous doctrine that "if lust leads to temptation, and Jesus was tempted, then Jesus lusted! To quote the apostle Paul, May it never be! Jesus could not sin. He was tempted to prove to man (whom He was here to save) that he could not be tempted. Dr. J. Vernon McGee has an excellent illustration to demonstrate this:

One year a flood washed out the wooden bridge on which the Santa Fe railroad crossed the river. They replaced it with a steel bridge, and when they completed it, they brought in two locomotives, stopped them on top of the bridge, and tied down both of the whistles. All of us who lived in that little town knew that something was happening. We ran down to see what it was-all twenty-three of us! When we got there, one of the braver citizens asked the engineer, "what are you doing?" The engineer replied, "Well, we built this bridge, and we are testing it." The man asked, "Why? Do you think it's going to fall down?" That engineer drew himself up to his full height and said, "Of course it won't fall down! We are proving it won't fall down." For the same reason, Jesus was tested to prove to that you and I have a savoir who could not sin. God cannot be tempted with sin, and God will not tempt you with sin.[33]"

Now to examine verse 15.

> Then when lust has conceived, it gives birth to sin; and when sin is accomplished, it brings forth death.

The word used translated here as *conceived* means, quite literally, "to become pregnant." James is saying that our old nature is bursting out, and uniting with lust to bring forth sin! The progression can be traced as follows:

1. Lust leads to temptation.

2. Temptation may lead to sin.

---

[33] McGee, J. Vernon. *Through the Bible Vol. 5.* 634

3. Sin leads to death.

Parallel this with 1 Peter 1:6-9

⁶In this you greatly rejoice, though now for a little while, if need be, you have been grieved by various trials,

Peter is establishing that, even though there are persecutions, even though there are trials, we can rejoice in them, knowing that we have an inheritance waiting us. Remember, when Peter wrote this epistle, Nero was savagely murdering Christians the length and breadth of his empire! And their deaths were horribly gruesome. Verse six tells us that there is hope, and the next verse helps explain why this suffering is necessary.

⁷that the genuineness of your faith, being much more precious than gold that perishes, though it is tested by fire, may be found to praise, honor, and glory at the revelation of Jesus Christ,

Trails prove the genuineness of our faith. And our faith is precious to our God. More precious than earthly Gold or silver. Those things perish and fade through the fire. But, like our inheritance that is kept incorruptible in heaven, so to is our faith incorruptible. If we weather these trials, even though our bodies wither and fade, our faith remains. And this expresses our love to our Father! We have nothing to offer Him. Our good works are insufficient. We are saved by Grace alone. But through faith we can express our love. Remember, the world ridiculed, taunted, tortured, and killed Jesus. How can we, being human, offer less than He. Especially when we, being human, have an imperfect nature. A sin nature. Now to examine verse 8:

> ⁸whom having not seen you love. Though now you do not see Him, yet believing, you rejoice with joy inexpressible and full of glory,

Peter was writing to men who had not known Jesus personally, as He had. They had only faith to base their beliefs on. And yet, they did believe! They suffered...but they believed. The endured the trials. And they would rejoice, knowing that they had been found worthy to suffer, as had their Lord. And this faith would culminate in the promises given in earlier verses. And if that was insufficient to explain what would come at the end of their trials, Peter spells it out exactly for them in Verse 9.

> ⁹receiving the end of your faith—the salvation of your souls.

Remember that the recipients of this letter were men who had been scattered by the empire. Men who had citizenship in no particular place. They were aliens among the citizens of Asia Minor. But they were all citizens of heaven. Just as we are today. These verses give us hope. These verses give us purpose. They can be applied to believers today as readily as to the original recipients.

Now examine the progression of testing, as opposed to temptation:

1. Testing produces endurance.

2. Endurance produces faith (perfection).

3. Faith leads to Life.

When examined in this manner, it is easy to see that where temptation leads to death, trials, or, specifically, endurance while undergoing trials, leads to eternal life!

Soteriology
Chapter Nine

Essential elements

There is only one way to heaven. Scripture tells us in the gospel of John 14:6 that:

> I am the way, and the truth, and the life; no one comes to the Father, But through me.

So obviously there is no way to heaven except through Jesus. But how do we get there? Many denominations hope to gain admittance to heaven through their individual good works, or, if you are catholic, maybe through the "pool" of good works laid up by the saints. But this writer believes (as did the apostle Paul) that good works are insufficient to get to heaven. Romans 3:23 tells us:

> For all have sinned and fall short of the glory of God.

How then shall we get to heaven? Ephesians 2:8 tells us:

> For by grace you have been saved through faith; and that not of yourselves, it is the gift of God; not as a result of works, lest any man should boast.

If we are not saved by works, but by grace, then what must one do to be saved? What do you need to believe? 1 Corinthians 15:3-7 sums it up quite neatly.

> [3]For I delivered to you as of first importance what I also received, that Christ died for our sins according to the Scriptures, [4]and that He was buried, and that He was raised on the third day according to the Scriptures, [5]and that He appeared to Cephas, then to the twelve. [6]After that He appeared to more than five hundred brethren at one time, most of whom remain until now, but some have fallen asleep; [7]then He appeared to James, then to all the apostles; [8]and last of all, as to one untimely born, He appeared to me also.

Careful study of the 1 Corinthians 15 passage clearly identifies the following elements. That is, these are the things necessary for salvation. One must believe and acknowledge the following:

1. That you are a sinner.

2. That Jesus was who he said He was, that is, the Son of God, and God Himself.

3. That Jesus died for your sins, the perfect, eternal sacrifice.

4. That He rose again, and ascended into heaven.

We are saved by grace. It is a free gift. All one need do is believe.

Dispensational elements

The elements necessary for a believer's salvation has been discussed in the preceding section of this chapter. But what saved the Old Testament saints? In chapter two, this writer stated that the doctrine of dispensationalism was to broad in scope to be limited to a single area of theology. And so it is. A careful examination of the various dispensations is the best way to answer this question. Dr. Charles Ryrie gives the dispensational position in his classic work *DISPENSATIONALISM*:

> [34]This dispensationalist's answer to the question of the relation of grace and law is this: The basis of salvation in every age is the death of Christ; the requirement for salvation in every age is faith; the content of faith changes in the various dispensations.

---

[34] Ryrie, Charles. *DISPENSATIONALISM*, 115

Dr. Ryrie makes it clear that the basis for salvation in every era is Christ's death. But he asks how much about Christ was understood by the Old Testament saints. Further, what was the point of the sacrifices under the Mosaic system? His conclusion follows:

> In examining salvation under the Mosaic Law the principal question is simply, How much of what God was going to do in the future did the Old Testament believer comprehend.? According to both Old and New Testament revelation it is impossible to say that he saw the same promise, the same savior as we do today. Therefore, the dispensationalist's distinction between the content of his faith and the content of ours is valid. The basis of salvation is always the death of Christ; the means is always faith; the Object is always God (though mans understanding of God before and after the Incarnation is obviously different); but the content of faith depends on the particular revelation God was pleased to give at a certain time. These are the distinctions necessitated by plain interception of revelation as it was given.
>
> If by "ways" of salvation is meant different content of faith, then dispensationalism does teach various "ways" because the Scriptures reveal differing contents for faith in the progressive nature of God's revelation to mankind. But if by "ways" is meant more than one basis or means of salvation, then dispensationalism most emphatically does not teach more than one way, for salvation has been, is, and always will be based on the substitutionary death of Jesus Christ.

It has been said that believers of all ages are saved in the same manner. The Mosaic Law required that the Jews follow a system of sacrifices and tithes. Adherence to this system demonstrated their faith and obedience. They are saved as we are, by the death of Christ, but their requirements are different then ours.

Terms and definitions

Justification. To announce a favorable verdict. We are justified by the blood of Christ. This is a state that man is unable to reach on its own. It means that a state of righteousness is declared.

Sanctification. Ryrie defines the term as follows: God setting apart the believer for himself. Positionally at salvation, progressively throughout life, and ultimately when the believer arrives in His presence in heaven.[35]

Redemption. By His sacrifice on the cross, Jesus allows man to be redeemed, or purchased from eternal damnation. Christ's sacrifice was sufficient for all mankind, but applies only to those believing in His name. Another term that illustrates this important theological term is "set free."

Propitiation. The wrath of God, having been turned away, because of the Christ's sacrifice at Calvary.

Reconciliation. Sin is a chasm, which cannot be crossed by man alone. Sin separates man from God, because of the very nature of both man and the creator. Man is reconciled, or returned to fellowship, with God through the sacrifice, once and for all time, of Christ.

---

[35] Ryrie, Charles. *Basic Theology*, page 630.

Ecclesiology
Chapter Ten

Essential Elements

The Biblical church must follow the example of the New Testament teachings in that it will be comprised only of persons who have professed belief in Jesus Christ. These believers organize, unite, and meet regularly for worship and fellowship. The following scriptures demonstrate that it is comprised of regenerate, baptized believers.

> [38]Peter *said* to them, "Repent, and each of you be baptized in the name of Jesus Christ for the forgiveness of your sins; and you will receive the gift of the Holy Spirit.
>
> - Acts 2:38

> ²to the church of God which is at Corinth, to those who have been sanctified in Christ Jesus, saints by calling, with all who in every place call on the name of our Lord Jesus Christ, their *Lord* and ours:
> -1 Corinthians 1:2

> ¹Paul, an apostle of Christ Jesus by the will of God, To the saints who are at Ephesus and *who are* faithful in Christ Jesus: ²Grace to you and peace from God our Father and the Lord Jesus Christ.
> - Ephesians 1:1-2

These believers recognize Christ as the Church's Lord and Head. For a demonstration of this principle, see the following scriptures: Matthew 28:18-20; Ephesians 1:22-23, 3:10-11, and 5:23.

These believers recognize Scripture alone as rule for faith and practice. See the following scriptures:

> ¹⁶All Scripture is inspired by God and profitable for teaching, for reproof, for correction, for training in righteousness; ¹⁷so that the man of God may be adequate, equipped for every good work.
> - 2 Timothy 3:16

> ²preach the word; be ready in season *and* out of season; reprove, rebuke, exhort, with great patience and instruction.
> - 2 Timothy 4:2

> ¹⁶Let the word of Christ richly dwell within you, with all wisdom teaching and admonishing one another with psalms *and* hymns *and* spiritual

> spiritual songs, singing with thankfulness in your hearts to God.
>
> -Colossians 3:16

Organization

The local church is God's plan for this dispensation. It began on the day of Pentecost, when it was empowered by the Holy Spirit at Pentecost. There are two divinely appointed officers in a church. These are Elders and Deacons. Both of these offices must be elected by the local church in accordance with the qualifications established in the New Testament. The responsibilities of the Elder/s (also called pastor, bishop, teacher, preacher) are to preside over an assembly. To shepherd the flock. To preach, and to teach.

The responsibilities of the deacon is to assist the elders in spiritual and temporal matters. These responsibilities can be found in the books of Acts, Titus, and 1 Timothy.

Ordinances

The Church has been tasked with two ordinances, both of which are to be observed as a memorial. These are NOT sacraments, but are symbolic in nature. These ordinances are Baptism and Communion.

Baptism should be by immersion. Nothing else is scriptural. It symbolizes the new life of the believer as a result of his union with Christ. In order to qualify for baptism, a believer must have a strong understanding of what the ordinance means. The believer must be what is implied by the very name "believer", that is, he must be regenerate through a profession of Jesus Christ. Immersion was the only form of this ordinance that was practiced among the early church. The trouble began later, when, for health purposes, it became expedient to begin a new form, that of "pouring". But, as always, once you begin to make allowances for expediency, it becomes easier and easier to make even more drastic changes. And so the church transitioned to "sprinkling". But the only biblical form of the ordinance is immersion, and that is the form that should be practiced among believers today.

Communion (the Lord's Supper) is symbolic of the Lord's suffering and death. This ordinance is the cause of much diverse opinion among the church, and has been since the reformation.

Roman Catholic's subscribe to the Theory of Transubstantiation. This means that after the consecration the body and blood, together with the soul and divinity of our Lord, are contained "truly and substantially in the sacrament". The Priest supernaturally changes the Wine and wafer into the very body and blood of Jesus.

Lutherans believe in the theory of Consubstantiation. While they reject the idea that the Wine and Bread are supernaturally transformed, they do believe that the body and blood of Christ are supernaturally united with the bread and wine, so that they are received when the latter are.

Then there is the Zwinglian (or symbolic) method. This means that the act of communion is symbolic only, that it is to remind us of the sacrificial work of Jesus.

There are other controversies surrounding the Lord's Supper. When Jesus established the act, he used unleavened bread. Why? Because it was during the Passover, and that was the only type of bread to be had! Over the ages, various churches have split over the issue of leavened vs. unleavened. The Roman Catholics to this day use communion wafers, which are unleavened, while the Greek Orthodox use leavened.

The early church imitated the entire meal, and met for feast. Similar to modern church "potluck" meals. But what does this mean to the Bible-believing Christian today? Does it matter if he uses grape juice instead of wine? Is the type of bread used important? In the New Testament, the Gospels of Matthew, Mark, and Luke all record the Lord's Supper. In 1 Corinthians 11:24-26, Paul say the following: ...that the Lord Jesus in the night in which He was betrayed took bread; and when he had given thanks, he broke it, and said, "This is my body, which is for you; do this in remembrance of me." In the same way He took the cup also, after supper, saying, "This cup is the new covenant in my blood; do this, as often as you drink it, in remembrance of me."

Paul continues on in Verses 23-44; For as often as you eat this bread and drink the cup, you proclaim the Lord's death until He comes. Therefore whoever eats the bread and drinks the cup of the Lord in an unworthy manner, shall be guilty of the body and the blood of the Lord. But let a man examine himself, and so let him eat of the bread and drink of the cup. For he who eats and drinks, eats and drinks judgment to himself, if he does not judge the body lightly.

It was necessary for Paul to speak to the Corinthians as he did because of certain abuses, or excesses, that were taking place within the Corinthian church. We as believers must be careful not to imitate those same abuses.

Note: For a detailed examination of the various ecclesiastical governmental forms, doctrines, and practices, see AppendixB1. For an examination of the Church and the Crusades, but especially the First Crusade, as well as the Knight's Templar, see Appendix B2.

Eschatology
Chapter Eleven

Sequence of Events

The next major even to occur that God has prophesied will be Christ's rapture of His bride, the church. This event is imminent and will occur before the tribulation and millennial events in time. At the rapture Christ will personally return in the air and receive all believers of this dispensation, both alive and dead, and give them glorified bodies as He takes them with Himself to heaven. This will be a bodily resurrection of the believers who have died and a bodily translation of living believers. In addition to 1 Thessalonians 1:10, which follows, see the following scriptures for an illustration of these events: Philippians 3:20; 1 Thessalonians 4:13-18; 1 Thessalonians 5:1-10;

I Corinthians 15:48-57; and Titus 2:13.

> [10]and to wait for His Son from heaven, whom He raised from the dead, *that is* Jesus, who rescues us from the wrath to come.
> - 1Thessalonians 1:10

Scripture teaches that the church saints will be in heaven during the seven years following the Rapture. They will all stand before the Bema (or Judgment seat of Christ) to receive rewards in accordance with their works as believers in this life. The will then be gathered to the marriage supper of the Lamb. In addition to the scripture presented below, see the following scriptures as evidence: 1 Corinthians 3:12-15; and Revelation 19:7-8.

> [10]For we must all appear before the judgment seat of Christ, so that each one may be recompensed for his deeds in the body, according to what he has done, whether good or bad.
> - 2 Corinthians 5:10

The rapture of the church does not signal the beginning of the tribulation. The signing of a treaty between the antichrist and Israel signals the beginning of the tribulation. The tribulation is the seven year period during which God will pour out unprecedented judgment upon the ungodly in general, and upon Israel in particular, so that Israel will turn to the Lord, receive Him and be saved. See the following scriptures: Daniel 7:25-27, 9:24-27; Jeremiah 30:7; 1 Thessalonians 5:1-9; and Revelation 6:1-9.

The tribulation will end with the personal and visible return of Christ to the earth. This will end the Times of the Gentiles and the nations of the world are defeated and judged. Christ will then establish His kingdom upon earth as Israel is restored to the land. Satan will be bound; Old Testament and tribulation saints will then be resurrected and world wide peace and righteousness will then occur.

Major Eschatological Events

1. Christ's return. This will take place at the end of the Great Tribulation. That is, at the end of the second three and a half year period. In addition to the scriptures presented below, see Zechariah 14:4; Isaiah 11:14; Matthew 24:29-31; and Revelation 19:11-16.

   > [25]"There will be signs in sun and moon and stars, and on the earth dismay among nations, in perplexity at the roaring of the sea and the waves, [26]men fainting from fear and the expectation of the things which are coming upon the world; for the powers of the heavens will be shaken. [27]"Then they will see THE SON OF MAN COMING IN A CLOUD with power and great glory. [28]"But when these things begin to take place, straighten up and lift up your heads, because your redemption is drawing near."
   >
   > - Luke 21:25-28

2. Times of the Gentiles ends. This is the end of the period of gentile domination over Israel, and it is definitely the end of the antichrist. See the following scriptures: Daniel 2:44, 7:25-27; Luke 21:24.

3. Christ's Kingdom established. In addition to the scripture presented, see Zechariah 14:9-11; and Revelation 11:15-17.

   > [13]"I kept looking in the night visions, And behold, with the clouds of heaven One like a Son of Man was coming, And He came up to the Ancient of Days And was presented before

> Him. ¹⁴"And to Him was given dominion, Glory and a kingdom, That all the peoples, nations and *men of every* language Might serve Him. His dominion is an everlasting dominion Which will not pass away; And His kingdom is one Which will not be destroyed.
>
> - Daniel 7:13-14

4. Satan bound. At this time, Satan will be bound, and cast into a pit for the duration of the millennial kingdom.

   > ¹Then I saw an angel coming down from heaven, holding the key of the abyss and a great chain in his hand. ²And he laid hold of the dragon, the serpent of old, who is the devil and Satan, and bound him for a thousand years; ³and he threw him into the abyss, and shut *it* and sealed *it* over him, so that he would not deceive the nations any longer, until the thousand years were completed; after these things he must be released for a short time.
   >
   > - Revelation 20:1-3

5. Resurrection and righteousness reigns. After the events described above, the kingdom will be established, and will reign everlasting. See Isaiah 65:18-25; and Zechariah 14:16-21.

After the Millennial Kingdom, Satan will be loosed for a little season and deceive the nations again. Multitudes will make one final revolt against Christ, but will be defeated along with Satan. The unregenerate dead of all time will be resurrected to stand at the Great White Throne Judgment where each will be justly, condemned eternally to the lake of fire where Satan and his followers have been cast. True believers of all ages will then enjoy eternal blessedness in the presence of their Creator and Savior in a new heaven and new earth where only righteousness is found for evermore.

A countdown to the end of Daniel's 69th Week[36]

Gabriel begins his message with some numbers that are vitally important for us to understand. He tells Daniel, "Seventy 'sevens' are decreed four your people." Another version says "Seventy weeks." Most of us know what a week is, but if we think this means a week of days, it won't work. In the Old Testament, (sometimes) the week refers to seven years, not seven days.

One proof of this is in Leviticus where it says, "for six years sow your fields, and for six years prune your vineyards and gather their crops. But in the seventh year the land is to have a Sabbath of rest, a Sabbath to the Lord" Lev. 25:3-4). We know about the Sabbath day, but here the Bible teaches us about the Sabbath year. The Jewish people were told to count off seven Sabbaths of years (seven times seven years) and then there was to be the year of Jubilee. The week of years was a part of the Old Testament culture, so Daniel must have been mentally calculating the time frame that Gabriel gave him.

The prophecy of the seventy weeks has to do with 490 years. Until this time, we have seen God's prophecies concerning the Gentile rulers and nations. Now He says, "I haven't forgotten you, Jews. I have cut out of the calendar 490 years that belong to you, and I'm going to show you how my program is going to work in that period of time."

If weeks are years, how long is a year? Most of us would answer "A year is 365 days, of course." No, it isn't. In the Old Testament, the prophetic year was 360 days long. The account

---

[36] Adapted from Dr. David Jeremiah's *The handwriting on the wall*, chapter 15.

of the Genesis flood gives us the mathematical reasoning behind the days in the year.

In Genesis 7 we are told that the flood began on the seventeenth day of the second month and ended on the seventeenth day of the seventh month. So the flood lasted for five months, didn't it? In the same chapter it say's that the waters flooded the earth for 150 days. Simple division will show us that the months were 30 days in duration, and 12 months times 30 days equals 360 days, which was the length of the Jewish year.

Scholars such as Sir Robert Anderson and Harold Hoehner have converted the 360-day Jewish calendar into our 365-day calendar, and when all the information was inserted into the equation the conclusion as the same. Perhaps you are thinking, "What happened to the other five days?" We don't have a perfect calendar, so we have what we call leap year. The Jews did the same thing, which we'll find out about later. However, their leap year was a bigger leap year than ours.

[37]Daniel 9:25 states that the starting point of the seventy weeks is the issuance of a command to restore and rebuild Jerusalem. Daniel was told by the angel, "Know and understand this: From the issuing of the decree to restore and rebuild Jerusalem until the Anointed One, the ruler, comes, there will be seven 'sevens' and sixty-two 'sevens.' It will be rebuilt with streets and a trench, but in times of trouble."

To start God's time clock again, we need to look at Nehemiah Chapter 2. Nehemiah was a man of great faith and prayer who led the third return of the exiles to Jerusalem. Two major expeditions had already made the long journey After Cyrus had given them their freedom.

---

[37] Jeremiah, David. Chapter 16

> [1]And it came to pass in the month of Nisan, in the twentieth year of King Artaxerxes, when wine was before him, that I took the wine and gave it to the king. Now I had never been sad in his presence before.
> - Nehemiah 2:1

This was the date that the King made his decree. Artaxerxes began to reign in 465 B.C. and so the twentieth year of his reign would have been 445 B.C. The first day of Nisan is March 14, 445 B.C. We need to remember that weeks are counted as years, and the years had 360 days. Simple calculation of this time element is this: 69 weeks (of years) x 7 (days in the week) = 483 x 360 (days in the year) = 173,800. Now if you take March 14, 445 B.C., and add to it 173,800 days, you come to April 6, A.D. 32. According to Sir Robert Anderson in his chronology, it was on that day the Jesus Christ rode into the city on His triumphal entry.

Major Tribulational Viewpoints

Within the evangelical church, there are two main theological viewpoints: Dispensational, and Covenantal. Each viewpoint has its own central position on eschatology, and within each central viewpoint there are divisions. Within the Dispensational viewpoint known as premillennialism, there are at least three such divisions! Then there are the Amillennial and Post-millennial views..

Dr. Thomas Ice describes the Amillennial view as follows:

> According to Amillennialism, there will be no literal, future 1000-year reign of Christ on earth; however, it usually holds that there is a

present spiritual form of the kingdom. The English theological term is made up of the following elements: *a* is from the Greek and means "no". *Mille* and *annus* are Latin and mean "thousand" and "years" respectively.

Amillennialism teaches that from the ascension of Christ in the first century until His second coming both good and evil will increase in the world as God's kingdom parallels Satan's kingdom. (There is no rapture.) Even though it believes that Satan is currently bound, it teaches that evil increases. When Jesus Christ returns, the end of the world will occur with a general resurrection and general judgment of all people. This view is essentially a spiritualization of the kingdom prophecies.

Amillennialism was not present in the earliest church; at least there is no positive record of its existence. It appears to have risen first as a result of opposition to premillennial literalism and then later, developed into a positive system. Amillennialism came to dominate the church when the great church father and theologian Augustine (354-430) abandoned premillennialism in favor of Amillennialism. It is no exaggeration to say that among the church's leadership (including the majority of protestant reformers during the fifteenth and sixteenth centuries) amilennialism has been the most widely held view for much of the church's history.[38]

Dr. Ice sums up postmillennialism as well:

Postmillennialism teaches that Christ's kingdom is now being extended throughout the

---

[38] Ice, Thomas. *Fast Facts on Bible Prophecy*. 12-13

world through the preaching of the gospel. It states that a majority of inhabitants will be converted to Christ, resulting in a consequent Christianization of the current world's society. Postmillennialism relates to the second coming of Christ to the earth "after the thousand years."

Postmillennialism teaches that the current age is the millennium, which is not necessarily a literal thousand years. Postmillennialists believe that through spiritual means there will be progressive growth of righteousness, prosperity, and development in every sphere of life as a growing majority of Christians eventually subdue the world for Christ. Then, after Christianity has dominated the world for a long time (the church's glorious reign of victory), Christ will return. At this time, like amillennialism, postmillennialism teaches that there will be a general resurrection, destruction of this present creation, and entry into the eternal state. Postmillennialism differs from premillennialism and amillennialism in that it optimistically believes that this victory will be realized without the need for a cataclysmic return of Christ to impose righteousness. Rather, victory will result from faithful application of means available during our present age. Postmillennialism did not really develop into a distinct system of eschatology until after the reformation. Prior to that time there was development of various elements that later were included into the theological mix of modern postmillennialism. Postmillennialism was the last major millennial position to develop.[39]

---

[39] Ice, Thomas. 150-151.

Premillennialists believe that the Lord Jesus will return for His church before the millennium. The millennium will last for a literal thousand years, followed by the final judgment, and the creation of the new heaven and new earth. The major point of disagreement within the premillennial family involves the rapture. At this point it becomes necessary to discuss the doctrine of the rapture. The theological definition is very different from common English usage. As used in regular conversation, the term usually refers to physical or spiritual ecstasy. Defined theologically, it is the term used to describe the removal of the church from the earth, into heaven. While the term itself cannot be found in scripture, the Greek word translates as "caught up". Thus, believers will be caught up into the heavens when called by Jesus Christ.

The passages which describe this doctrine are found throughout the New Testament. 1 Thessalonians 4:16 –17 are considered to be THE classic rapture passages:

> [16]For the Lord Himself will descend from heaven with a shout, with the voice of an archangel, and with the trumpet of God. And the dead in Christ will rise first. [17]Then we who are alive and remain shall be caught up together with them in the clouds to meet the Lord in the air. And thus we shall always be with the Lord.

The Greek word for the term "caught up" is ἁρπαγησόμεθα. *Strong's exhaustive Concordance of the Bible* defines the term as follows:

> From a derivative of G138; to *seize* (in various applications):—catch (away, up), pluck, pull, take (by force).

Paul gives us more information in 1 Corinthians 15:51-52:

> ^{51}Behold, I tell you a mystery: We shall not all sleep, but we shall all be changed—^{52}in a moment, in the twinkling of an eye, at the last trumpet. For the trumpet will sound, and the dead will be raised incorruptible, and we shall be changed.

Dr. Walvoord's and Zuck's immense Bible Knowledge Commentary says the following about the 1 Corinthians 15:51-52:

> **15:51-52.** Paul had revealed the same truth to the Thessalonians (1Thessalonians 4:15-17). The Rapture of the church was a **mystery** (*mysteôrion*) in that it had not been known in the Old Testament but now was revealed. (Cf. other "mysteries"—now revealed truths—in Matt. 13:11; Luke 8:10; Rom. 11:25; 16:25; 1 Cor. 4:1; Eph. 1:9; 3:3-4, 9; 5:32; Col. 1:26-27; 2:2; 4:3; 2 Thes. 2:7; 1 Tim. 3:9, 16; Rev. 1:20; 10:7; 17:5.) The dead in Christ will first be raised, and then the living will be instantaneously transformed. The **trumpet,** as in the Old Testament, signaled the appearance of God (cf. Ex. 19:16). It is the last blast for the church because this appearance shall never end (cf. 1 Cor. 13:12). (There is no basis for posttribulationists equating this trumpet with the seventh trumpet in Rev. 11:15-19. The trumpets in Rev. pertain to judgments during the

> Tribulation, whereas the trumpet in 1 Cor. 15:52 is related to the church.[40])

So the rapture is the event in which God will remove His church from the earth, in order for events to unfold which will allow Israel to finish her history in triumph. If the church were on the earth, then the ultimate victory would still be God's, but through the church, rather than through His chosen people, Israel. This would violate covenant promises made to Israel, and is therefore not possible. The writer holds to the premillennial position, because this is the only viewpoint that a strict literal, grammatical, and historical hermeneutic will allow.

As was previously stated, there are three main positions within the premillennial viewpoint (Dr. Ryrie adds a fourth). They are Pretribulational; Midtribulational; Posttribulational; and Partial. The difference between the first three and the fourth is best defined by Dr. Charles Ryrie, "Partial rapture concerns the extent of the rapture, whereas the other three views focus on the time of the rapture[41]."

The pre-tribulation position teaches that the rapture will occur before the seven year tribulation will begin. This is the position held by this writer, as well as such eminent theologians as John N. Darby, John Walvoord, Dwight Pentecost, and Marvin Lubenow. It is supported in the scriptures in revelation 3:10:

> [10]Because you have kept My command to persevere, I also will keep you from the hour of trial which shall come upon the whole world, to test those who dwell on the earth.

---

[40] Walvoord and Zuck. *The Bible knowledge Commentary: New Testament.* 545-546

[41] Ryrie, Charles. *Basic Theology*, page 557

The *Bible Knowledge commentary* offers the following on this verse:

> **3:10.** The church in Philadelphia received no rebuke from Christ. Instead they were commended and given a promise because they had been willing to **endure patiently.** The promise was, **I will also keep you from the hour of trial that is going to come upon the whole world to test those who live on the earth.** This is an explicit promise that the Philadelphia church will not endure the hour of trial which is unfolded, beginning in Revelation 6. Christ was saying that the Philadelphia church would not enter the future time of trouble; He could not have stated it more explicitly. If Christ had meant to say that they would be preserved *through* a time of trouble, or would be *taken out* from within the Tribulation, a different verb and a different preposition would have been required. Though scholars have attempted to avoid this conclusion in order to affirm posttribulationism, the combination of the verb "keep" (*teôrein*) with the preposition "from" (*ek*) is in sharp contrast to the meaning of keeping the church "through" (*dia*), a preposition which is not used here. The expression "the hour of trial" (a time period) makes it clear that they would be kept *out of* that period. It is difficult to see how Christ could have made this promise to this local church if it were God's intention for the entire church to go through the Tribulation that will come on the entire world. Even though the church at Philadelphia would go to glory via death long before the time of trouble would come, if the church here is taken to be typical of

the body of Christ standing true to the faith, the promise seems to go beyond the Philadelphia church to all those who are believers in Christ (cf. Walvoord, *Revelation*, pp. 86-8)[42].

Based on this verse, it is not possible for the church to remain during the tribulation period described by the Prophet Daniel and the Apostle John. Those holding to the mid-tribulational viewpoint have interpreted the seventh week of Daniel to consist of only the last 3.5 years. Thus, they can claim to be pre-trib, but only when a different definition is applied to the term!

Those holding to a post-trib viewpoint do so on either the belief that both the rapture and the Second Coming are the same event, or that the rapture will occur just moments before the Second Coming, thus allowing the church to participate with Christ in the glorious appearing.

While the early church was premillennial, there was a shift from the time of Augustan until the 1800's. One of the major reasons for the shift had to do with the make up of the church. The early church was comprised primarily of Jewish believers. As time passed, however, the make up shifted primarily to gentile believers. Technically, these terms are incorrect, because scripture teaches that there is neither Jew nor Greek in Christ, but the distinction will suffice for my purposes here. As the gentile influence became stronger and stronger, it became apropos to blame the Jews for the death of Christ. And if the Jews were responsible for the rejection and death of the messiah, then it becomes obvious that the Jews were not God's chosen ones. And if this is true, then what can one do with all of the prophecies in the Old Testament concerning the Day of the Lord and such? Simple. If the church is God's chosen

---

[42] Walvoord and Zuck. 939-940

instrument in this age, all one must do is extend this age all the way back to the Abrahamic covenant. In point of fact, church's with covenantal doctrine place the beginning of the church with Abraham. If the church had replaced Israel in the eyes of God, then it is only natural to assume that the church would not need to be removed in order to fulfill the prophecies concerning Israel. And so the doctrine switched from premellinnial to Amillennial.

We have examined the three rapture viewpoints. Now we will examine the partial rapture view. Dr. Thomas ice describes this view as follows:

> [43]This view teaches that the rapture occurs before the tribulation, but only spiritual Christians will be taken. Other Christians will remain to be purified through the trials of the tribulation. Some versions teach multiple raptures throughout the tribulation.

Again, this view does not take a literal view of the rapture scriptures that have been previously examined. One must spiritualize scripture in order to make them fit! And there is no indication that these scriptures were intended to be figurative. And so one must apply a literal hermeneutic if one is to get a consistent, intelligible interpretation. To this point, the major Tribulational views have been defined and examined. In order to fully understand the various viewpoints, there are four methods of interpretation that must be looked at. These are the Historicist, the Preterist, the Futurist, and the Idealist.

---

[43] Ice, Thomas. 148

In his book Fast Facts on Bible Prophecy, Dr. Timothy Ice defines Historicism as follows:

> Historicism is one of the four possible interpretive views regarding the role of timing in Bible prophecy. It addresses the interpretive question, "When will a prophecy be fulfilled in history?" The four views reflect the four possibilities in relation to time: past (preterism), present (historicism0, future (futurism), and timeless (idealism).
>
> Historicism equates the current church age with the tribulation period through the day/year theory. The day/year theory takes numbers such as the 2,300 days (Daniel 8:14) and 1,290 days (Daniel 12;11) and declares them to be years. Thus, if one can find the right starting year it is merely a matter of adding the 2,300 or 1,290 years to discover the date of Christ's return. In addition, historicists also relate the seal, trumpet and bowl judgements to major historical events. For example, the fifth seal in Revelation 6 may be identified as the martyrdom under Roman Emperor Diocletian (A.D. 284-304). If that is true, then one might view the French Revolution as the first five bowl judgements of Revelation 16. This approach, coupled with Mormonism, Seventh-day Adventism, and Jehovah Witnesses.[44]the day/year theory naturally leads to date setting. Historicism was almost unanimously held by Protestant's from the reformation to about 100 years ago. It is also the view of many of religious groups started in the nineteenth century, such as

---

[44] Ice, Thomas. 48-49

While it might appear to be the method of choice for the purveyor of a literal hermeneutic, one must always beware of date setting. While scripture accurately set the date for Christ's triumphal entry into Jerusalem, it does not set the date so easily for His return. Strict date setting can lead to disastrous consequences within the church. Granted that the Jehovah's Witnesses are a cult, but one can only grieve for the hundreds of thousands who anticipated the return of Jesus Christ in the seventies, to the point of amassing huge debts in anticipation of being raptured out of repayment!

We turn again to Dr. Ice for a definition of the Preterist view.

> Preterism addresses the interpretive question, "When will a prophecy be fulfilled in history?"
>
> The preterists teach that most, if not all, prophesy has already been fulfilled. They argue that major prophetic portions of scripture (such as the Olivet discourse and the book of Revelation) were fulfilled in events surrounding the A.D. 70 destruction of Jerusalem by the Romans. They believe they are compelled to take such a view because Matthew 24:34 and its parallel passages say that "this generation shall not pass away until all these things take place." They argue that this means it had to take place in the first century.. Revelation, they advocate, says something similar in the passages that say Christ is coming "quickly" or that His return is "at hand." Having settled in their minds that these prophecies had to take place in the first century, they believe they are justified in making the rest of the language fit into a local (Jerusalem), instead of a worldwide fulfillment.

There are three kinds of preterism. For lack of better terms, we will call them *mild*, *moderate*, and *extreme*.

Mild preterists believe that the past fulfillment occurred during the first three centuries as God waged war on the two early enemies of the church: Israel and Rome. Israel was defeated in A.D. 70 and Rome in the fourth century.

Moderate preterists believe that almost all prophecy was fulfilled in the A.D. 70 event, but they believe that a few passages still teach a future second coming (Acts 1:9-11; 1 Corinthians 15:51-53; 1 Thessalonians 4:16, 17).

Extreme preterists, or *consistent* preterists as they prefer to be known, believe that all Bible prophecy was fulfilled in the destruction of Jerusalem in A.D. 70. They believe that if there is a future second coming the Bible doesn't talk about it.[45]

In order to make this system work, one must adhere rigorously to some scripture, while ignoring others. It is certainly not consistent, and leaves much to the individual to interpret.

Of the two remaining views, one holds to a completely non-literal view, and the other is the only approach that is truly consistent with the literal, grammatical, and historical hermeneutic. Idealism teaches that Revelation is a figurative book, and so must be interpreted in the same fashion. While it is true that much of revelation is allegorical in nature, and also true that apocalyptic writings are, by their very nature difficult to interpret, it is certainly neither true, nor consistent, to

---

[45] Ice, Thomas. 154-155

attempt to completely assign a allegorical hermeneutic to an entire book., simply because it is difficult to understand.

Futurism separates the church age from the 70th week, and assigns specific roles to both the church and corporate Israel. It combines the best features of historicism and preterism, and allows for a consistent hermeneutic.

It can be easily observed how these four methods can apply to the greater viewpoints. For instance, if one holds to the Amillennial view, then it is obvious that the futurist view cannot be ones interpretive method of choice. By the same token, if one holds to the premillennial position, then the idealist, preterist, and historicist positions become untenable.

This author holds to the premillennial, pretribulational position. Additionally, this author is a futurist when interpreting prophesy from Isaiah, Daniel, Zechariah, and Revelation. The Amillennial position doesn't hold to a consistent position on Israel, and smacks to this writer of anti-Semitism. The postmillennial position is almost dead, although its adherents seem to be blissfully unaware of this.

Appendixes

A. Paul, Model of a missionary

B1. Research on ecclesiastical governmental forms, doctrines, and practices

B2. The Church and the crusades; The Knight's Templar

C. Exegetical Word Study: Babylon

D. Selected Bibliography

Appendix A
Paul, Model of a missionary

At Stephen the Deacon's stoning, we get a glimpse of the man who began as an enemy of the early church, but who ended up as THE apostle to the gentiles. When we are introduced to him, he is called Saul. In Acts 8:1 we learn that he went from house to house, rousting out all Christ's faithful ones, and tossing them into jail.

> [1]Saul was in hearty agreement with putting him to death. And on that day a great persecution began against the church in Jerusalem, and they were all scattered throughout the regions of Judea and Samaria, except the apostles. [2]Some devout men buried Stephen, and made loud lamentation over him. [3]But Saul began ravaging the church, entering house after house, and

dragging off men and women, he would put them in prison.

While the Church scattered, and Philip evangelized, Saul decided that persecuting the church at Jerusalem was insufficient. He requested, and received, permission to persecute the church in Damascus. The high priest authorized Saul to arrest believers there, and to bring them to Jerusalem for trial.

But the Lord had other plans for Saul of tarsus. As Saul was made the arduous journey, while on the road to Damascus (Sounds like a Crosby/Hope musical), he was struck blind by a brilliant light from heaven and heard a voice calling him., saying "Saul, Saul, Why do you persecute me?" Jesus instructed to seek out a believer named Ananias in Damascus who would tell him what to do.

Ananias ministered to Saul, who received his sight and the Holy Spirit. Saul receive the power of the Holy Spirit, and began to preach of the One he had persecuted. He preached mightily, and soon the Jewish leaders, being outraged both by his conversion and success, decided to kill him. (Sound familiar?) Saul escaped the city by being let down over the city wall in a large basket. You could say that the road to Damascus was a turning point in history. Because, while Paul was not the first to preach to the gentiles, he was going to be used mightily in that capacity!

Family and cultural background

Paul was uniquely qualified to perform this ministry. He was born a Jew in a family of Pharisees of the tribe of Benjamin in Tarsus of Cilicia, an important city, a university city, rich in education, and hub of commerce and that embraced both the Hellenistic spirit, and Roman politics.

> ⁶But perceiving that one group were Sadducees and the other Pharisees, Paul *began* crying out in the Council, "Brethren, I am a Pharisee, a son of Pharisees; I am on trial for the hope and resurrection of the dead!"
>
> - Acts 23:6

> ⁵circumcised the eighth day, of the nation of Israel, of the tribe of Benjamin, a Hebrew of Hebrews; as to the Law, a Pharisee;
>
> - Philippians 3:5

> ¹¹And the Lord *said* to him, "Get up and go to the street called Straight, and inquire at the house of Judas for a man from Tarsus named Saul, for he is praying,
>
> - Acts 9:11

Parson's Bible Atlas has this to say about the city of Tarsus:

> An ancient city situated on the banks of the Cydnus River, about 10 miles (16 km) from the coast of SE Asia Minor. The wealth of the city was secured by its position S of the Cilician Gates, a gorge through which passed the great trade route between Syria and Asia Minor. Roman expansion allowed Tarsus to gain a measure of independence under the Seleucids, which led to the subsequent Hellenization of the city. It was made capital of the province of Cilicia about 67 B.C., and became a leading center of Greek learning. In Roman times, its population may have reached 500,000.

Paul was born in Tarsus, among the minority of Jews who held Roman citizenship. It was an ideal environment for his education, where Western culture and learning conjoined with the thought and religion of the East.

Paul's parents named him Saul after the first king of Israel, who was of the same tribe. Scripture notes that he "was also called Paul" .He used his Roman name throughout his epistles.

From religious parents Paul received knowledge of the Law and Prophets and the Hebrew and Aramaic languages. This was outside of the norm, because Tarsus was not a Jewish city. Rather it had a Hellenistic flavor where the Greek was spoken and Greek literature and arts were cultivated. Even were he not a scholar of note, this would account for the apostle to the gentile's familiarity with Greek, the ordinary language of the ordinary citizens of Tarsus.

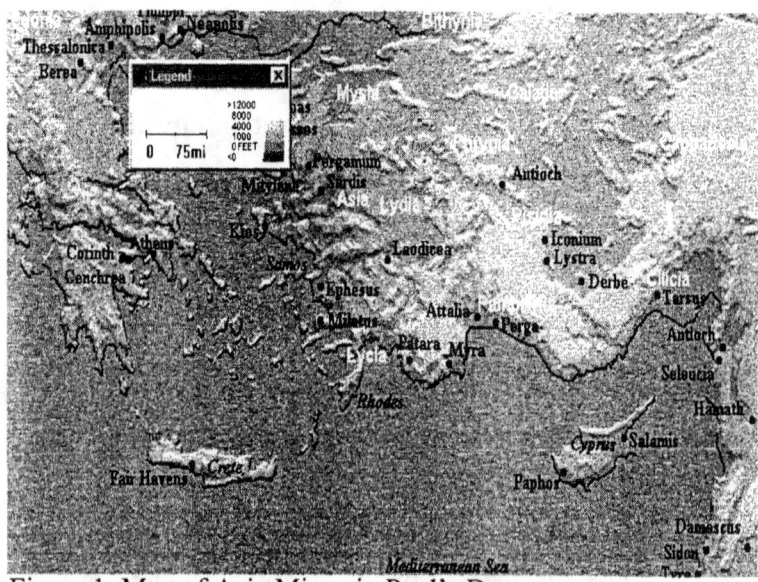

Figure 1. Map of Asia Minor in Paul's Day

Jews were originally brought to Tarsus, the capital of the Roman province of Cilicia, in 171 B.C., to promote commerce. It was during this period that Paul's ancestors probably became

Roman citizens. Paul would have inherited both Tarsisian and Roman citizenship from his father. These dual citizenship's would prove to be of great value to Paul throughout his adult life as he traveled, spreading the "good news" throughout the length and breadth of the Roman Empire!

It is possible that Paul had several brothers and sisters, (this would have been usual within a Jewish family), but Acts 23:16 mentions only one sister whose son performed a lifesaving act for his uncle.

> [16]But the son of Paul's sister heard of their ambush, and he came and entered the barracks and told Paul. [17]Paul called one of the centurions to him and said, "Lead this young man to the commander, for he has something to report to him."

In addition to his academic prowess, Paul was a tentmaker by vocation. It is unsure when or where he learned this trade, but he may have selected it as a means of self-support, as was the custom of those in rabbinic training. Tarsus was well known for the goat's hair cloth called *cilicium*. It was manufacture of this cloth and the fashioning of it into tents, sails, awnings, and cloaks that gave both the region its name, and Paul the freedom to preach without needing support from the body of Christ during his ministry.

Education

Although born in Tarsus, Paul testified to the Jews in Jerusalem that he had been "brought up in this city at the feet of Gamaliel" (Acts 22:3).

> [3]"I am a Jew, born in Tarsus of Cilicia, but brought up in this city, educated under Gamaliel,

strictly according to the law of our fathers, being zealous for God just as you all are today.

It is unclear at what point Paul was first brought to Jerusalem to begin his training, but it is likely that he began rabbinic training at about thirteen years of age. His teacher, was the famous Gamaliel, the grandson of the equally famous Hillel, who began the pharisaic school whose teachings run through the Talmudic writings to this day. (Note: This is the very Gamaliel whose wisdom persuaded the Sanhedrin to spare the lives of Peter and the apostles in Acts 5:33-40). It was while studying under that Paul began to advance in Judaism beyond many Jews of his own age (this was not uncommon, Jesus was extremely advanced at an even younger age!) and became extremely zealous for the traditions of his fathers.

Preparation for ministry

After Paul's conversion and escape from Damascus, he began a period of preparation, which lasted about thirteen years. During this time, Paul first was in the desert of Arabia for three years. Here was his opportunity to pray and reflect on Stephen's defense to the Sanhedrin, the momentous significance of is conversion, the vision he received of Jesus Christ, and the meaning of all this in the light of his rabbinical training. Paul then returned to Damascus visited the apostles Peter and James in Jerusalem.

At first the believers in Jerusalem were afraid, not believing that he was one of them. But Barnabas vouched for him, and he came to be accepted by the believers in Jerusalem. He was again forced to flee, and began his missionary journeys.

We can learn much from Paul. He shows us that God can use anyone, at anytime, to further His divine will. Paul was the most unlikely of candidates, and yet, he was uniquely prepared for ministry. Paul would claim that he "was all things to all peoples." Certainly no other apostle could make such a claim. His excellent rabbinical preparation opened the doors to the synagogues. His excellent Greek language skills, as well as knowledge of art and literature, made him an excellent minister to the Greeks! His Roman citizenship that he had been born with not that he had purchased, as the Centurion had done, both protected him as he traveled, and opened even more doors. So we can see that a divine call is necessary, and also that preparation is necessary. For if Paul had not studied, if he had not adequately prepared himself, he would not have been able to be "all things to all peoples!"

Appendix B1
Research on Ecclesiastical Governmental Forms, Doctrines, and Practices

Roman Catholic

The Pope today dominates the Roman Catholic Church. He has absolute control. This has been true since 1564, when the Bishop of Rome issued a Papal Bull at one of the sessions of the Council of Trent. Earle Cairns says the following about that council:

> The real significance of the council was the transformation of medieval Thomistic theology into an authoritative dogma binding on all the faithful. It rendered any chance of reconciliation with Protestantism impossible, because the Protestants would not accept the equal authority of tradition and scripture. It did, however,

promote a higher moral standard among the clergy by needed reforms. It opened seminaries to train ministers, provided for the Roman Catechism of 1566, and adopted an authoritative version of the Bible, the Vulgate. It marked the final defeat of conciliarism and the triumph of curial or papal absolutism.[46]

At the head of the Church is the Pope. The College of Cardinals selects him. Usually, but not always, he is elected from among the College. The Pope, from among the ranks of Archbishops, creates the Cardinals. Each Archbishop rules over a large area, divided into Bishoprics, which are singularly known as Diocese. Each Diocese is divided into parishes. A Monsignor oversees several parishes, which in turn are overseen by Priests. This may seem to be a convoluted system. It seems so because it is! Add to this the various Priestly orders, fraternal orders, and various orders for Nuns, and you can easily become confused.

How did the Catholic Church as described above, evolve from the early church model, given in the book of acts, and laid out by the apostle Paul in 1 and 2 Timothy, and Titus? It is easy to see how, in the beginning, it strived to follow the simpler forms of government. You had Pastors and Bishops over the believers in each city. The Bishops supervised the larger, metropolitan areas, and the Pastors governed the smaller churches within. Arguably, this seems to follow, at least loosely, the model of the Bible. But eventually, the bishop of Rome decided for several reasons that, to quote Orwell, while all animals are equal, some animals are more equal than others! In other words, the See of Rome was superior to all others, and all others were therefore subservient to the Bishop of Rome. Before this occurred, the bishops of the larger areas were affectionately known as "Papa". But from this point on, only

---

[46] Cairns, Earle E. *Christianity Through The Centuries*, page 346

the Bishop of Rome could use this name. Only the bishop of Rome could be referred to as "Pope".

The largest single area of difference between Catholicism and Protestantism is in reference to the doctrines of Sacraments and their effect upon individual Salvation. The Catholic Church maintains, and has maintained for centuries, that Salvation can only come through itself, through the administration of the sacraments. And furthermore, that the church should rightfully dominate the secular government. Perry Rogers has this to say:

> The struggle for supremacy between church and state had stirred such dissension in the eleventh and twelfth centuries, seemed settled by the strong leadership of Pope Innocent III in the early thirteenth century. Innocent simply dominated the secular world without a moment of hesitation. But conditions had changed by the late thirteenth century. The forceful kings of England and France were constantly in need of money and began levying taxes against the clergy of their realms. Boniface VIII (1294-1303), in the viewed this as an encroachment upon the liberty of the church.[47]

Boniface VII battled these problems with two significant Papal Bulls, Clericis Laicos (1298) and Unam Sanctam (1302), both of which stressed Papal supremacy. See Sections 6 and 7 to read these Decrees. The church believed, and indeed, continues to believe, in its supremacy, in both secular and spiritual arenas. As such, the Catholic Church does not support the idea of separation of church and state. Indeed, when the church is in the majority, it pushes for the exclusion of all other faiths. And when it is in the minority, it calls loudly for freedom of religion for all. This type of hypocrisy has led to a significant decline in membership within the church in modern

---

[47] Rogers, Perry M. *Aspects of Western Civilization*, Vol. I, 367

times. But the idea that there is only one way to heaven, controlled by the church alone, is a major point of division. However, if the Catholic Church is correct, and salvation does indeed come only through the church through administration of the sacraments, then the idea and practice of the inquisition is justified. Henry Vedder comments on this aspect in his book *A Short History of the Baptists*:

> Granting this doctrine of sacramental grace, not only is Rome justified in persecuting, but all who believe in sacramental grace are wrong not to persecute. For if salvation is impossible except through the church and its sacraments, every heretic is, as Rome charges, a murderer of souls. Is it not right to restrain and punish a murderer? From this point of view it becomes the duty of the church to root out heresy at all cost of human life-to make the world a desert, if need be, but at any rate to ensure peace. And all persecutors have been half-hearted in the work except only Rome, she has had the courage of her accursed convictions. She alone has recognized that if you say A you must also say B, and so on, to the end of the alphabet; that if you once begin to persecute you must not tremble at blood and tears nor shrink from sending men to the rack, the gibbet, and the stake. The inquisition is the perfectly logical, the inevitable outcome of Roman doctrine, and the entire system of persecution is rooted in this idea of sacramental grace.[48]

The problem then stems from the difference between what Protestants call Ordinances, and the Catholics call Sacraments. For the Roman Catholic, worship centers around the mass, which itself is centered on communion. In the Catholic service,

---

[48] Vedder, Henry C. *A Short History of the Baptists*. 98-99

the cup is withheld from the laity, and drunk entirely by the priest who celebrates the mass. The bread is then distributed to the congregation. The type of communion taught by the Catholic Church is Transubstantiation. This belief teaches that the wine and bread become the very body and blood of Christ. Salvation based on sacraments is temporary, and must be renewed periodically.

There were many dissidents within the Catholic Church to such unscriptural, high-handed tactics. These were dealt with through what ever means was necessary. One method was the Inquisition, another was intellectual, through the use of the index. The index was a list of banned books, including works by Thomas Paine, Erasmus, and other "subversives". The index was maintained, with books constantly being added, until 1966. Earle Cairns has the following to say about these methods:

> The Roman church had two weapons of coercion to back up the propaganda of the Jesuits. These were the Inquisition and the Index. The Inquisition had originated in the struggle against the Albigenses in southern France early in the thirteenth century. It had been established in Spain by Papal license in 1480 to deal with the problem of heresy in that land. Under Thomas Torquemada's (1420-98) leadership, ten thousand were executed; and under Ximinez, about two thousand died. Because of Caraffa's urging, the Roman Inquisition was proclaimed by a papal bull of Paul III in 1542 as an instrument to deal with heresy anywhere until the Inquisition was abolished in 1854. Those accused were always presumed guilty till they proved their innocence; they were punished by loss of property, imprisonment, or burning at the stake, unless they confessed and recanted. These punishments

were carried out by the secular authorities under the watchful eyes of the inquisitors.

The development of printing in the middle of the fifteenth century helped the Protestants to disseminate their ideas. To counteract this, the Roman church developed the Index, a list of books that the faithful were not permitted to read. As Paul IV, Caraffa issued the first Roman Index of Prohibited Books in 1559. The books of Erasmus and some Protestant editions of the Bible appeared on the list. A special Congregation of the Index, created in 1571, was charged by the Pope with the task of keeping the list up to date. he index kept many Roman Catholics from reading Protestant literature, and the Inquisition forced many to recant their Protestant views.[49]

The Roman Catholic Church did not take hold in North America easily. Since the original colonists were Puritans, and since once in America, those who fled religious persecution became persecutors themselves, Roman Catholic settlers were in the extreme minority. The colony of Maryland was originally founded for those of the Catholic faith, but even there, the religion found it necessary to keep a low profile. Earle Cairns says the following about the growth of Catholicism in America:

> Catholicism did not take root in the thirteen colonies until 1643 in Maryland. Most of the Irish and Germans who came after 1850 were Roman Catholic.
>
> The Lords Baltimore-George Calvert (ca. 1580-1632) and his son, Cecil Calvert (1605-75)-were successive proprietors of what became known as Maryland. Unlike the idealistic Roger Williams, the Calvert's were interested in

---

[49] Cairns, Earle E. *Christianity Through the Centuries*. 344 -345

profits. From 1634, when the colony began, they permitted religious toleration so that Protestants as well as Roman Catholics would settle there. The Strict political control by Calvert was balanced by religious toleration until Maryland was made a royal colony in 1692. Anglicanism became the established religion in 1702.[50]

Especially during the revolutionary period, because of the founding fathers insistence upon the separation of Church and State. Catholicism in North America would gain ground later, with the influx of Irish immigrants.

Baptist

Each Baptist congregation is fully autonomous. That is to say, they are not under any council, synod, or titular head. There are more Baptist variations than you can shake a stick at. Some of the larger denominations within the United States are: The Southern Baptist Convention (SBC), the Conservative Baptist Association (CBA), the Independent Fundamental Baptists. It has been said that there are more varieties of Baptists than any other denomination. The purpose of this paper is not to explain the subtle differences between these groups, but to point out, in general, how these bodies are governed. It has already been said that the government of the baptistic churches are autonomous and congregational. There is a story told about Lyndon B. Johnson and the Southern Baptist Convention. It seems that the leaders of the SBC didn't approve of LBJ drinking in the public spotlight, and threatened to excommunicate him if he continued. But LBJ would have none of that. He claimed he couldn't be excommunicated, because no one in the
SBC had the authority! The amusing thing is that, he was essentially correct! Only his home church could disfellowship him, the SBC can only make suggestions. (Not to mention the

---

[50] Cairns, Earle E. 363

fact that the term "excommunication" has no meaning to Protestants.)

The Baptististic churches in general recognize two ordinances. One is Baptism, and the other is the Lord's Supper. Baptism is fairly easy to address. Virtually all Baptists subscribe to the idea of believer baptism only, by method of full immersion. It is symbolic in that it represents the old man going down, with the new man coming up. Baptists do not believe in the idea of baptismal regeneration. The other methods of baptism, i.e., sprinkling and pouring, arose out of necessity, but have no scriptural representation. They are accepted by tradition.

In order to explain the Lord's Supper, it becomes necessary to give a brief explanation of the views held by the Lutheran's as well as the Romans. As mentioned earlier, the Roman Catholic's subscribe to the doctrine of Transubstantiation. This means that after the consecration the body and blood, together with the soul and divinity of our Lord, are contained "truly and substantially in the sacrament". The Priest supernaturally changes the Wine and wafer into the very body and blood of Jesus.

The Lutherans believe in the doctrine of Consubstantiation. While they reject the idea that the Wine and Bread are supernaturally transformed, they do believe that the body and blood of Christ are supernaturally united with the bread and wine, so that they are received when the latter are. Justo Gonzalez tries to explain the Lutheran doctrine:

> Luther rejected a great deal of commonly accepted doctrine regarding communion. He was particularly opposed to the celebration of private masses, to the understanding of communion as a repetition of the sacrifice at Calvary, to the notion that there are "merits" in the mass, to the doctrine of transubstantiation,

and to the "reservation" of the sacrament-the claim that the body of Christ remains present in the bread even after the celebration of communion is over. But, in spite of his opposition to what he saw as the misuse and misrepresentation of communion, he continued to attach great importance to the sacrament itself, and to the presence of Christ in it. While insisting on the need for the preached word, he retained the word made visible in communion as the center of Christian worship.

The question of the manner in which Christ is present in communion gave rise to long debates, not only with Catholics, but also among Protestants. Luther categorically rejected the doctrine of transubstantiation, which he saw as unduly tied to Aristotelian-and therefore pagan-metaphysics. Also, the manner in which the doctrine of transubstantiation had been used had tied it to the theory that the mass was a meritorious sacrifice, and this ran contrary to justification by faith.

On the other hand, Luther was not ready to reduce communion to a mere sign or symbol of spiritual realities. He took the words of Jesus at the institution of the sacrament as very clear and undeniable proof of his physical presence at the sacrament:: "this is my body." Therefore, Luther felt compelled to affirm that in communion believers truly and literally partake of the body of Christ. This need not imply, as with transubstantiation, that the bread becomes body, and the wine becomes blood. The bread is still bread, and the wine is still wine. But now the body and blood of the Lord are also in them, and the believer is nourished by that body and that blood through the very act of eating the

> bread and drinking the wine. Although later interpreters used the term "consubstantiation" to describe the presence of Christ in Communion, Luther never used such metaphysical terms, but would rather speak of the presence of the body of Christ in, with, under, around, and behind, the bread and wine. [51]

Baptist's in general adhere to the Zwinglian method. This means that the act of communion is symbolic only, that it is to remind us of the sacrificial work of Jesus.

There are other controversies surrounding the Lord's Supper. When Jesus established the act, He used unleavened bread. Why? Because it was during the Passover, and that was the only type of bread to be had! Over the ages, various churches have split over the issue of leavened vs. unleavened. The Roman Catholics to this day use communion wafers, which are unleavened, while the Greek Orthodox use leavened. The bottom line is that, to the Baptists at least, the elements don't much matter. The act is symbolic, and the Lord's Supper is held out of obedience.

Baptist churches in general follow the example of the New Testament teachings that the membership will be consisting only of persons who have professed belief in Jesus Christ. These believers organize, unite, and meet regularly for worship and fellowship. The local church is God's plan for this dispensation. It was formed during Jesus' earthly ministry, and was empowered by the Holy Spirit at Pentecost.

There are two divinely appointed officers in a church. These are Elder and Deacon. Both of The local church in accordance with the qualifications established must elect these offices in the New Testament. The responsibilities of the Elders (also called pastor, bishop, teacher, preacher. The words are used

---

[51] Gonzalez, Justo I. *The Story of Christianity Vol. II.* 35-36.

interchangeably in scripture.) are to preside over an assembly. To shepherd the flock, to preach, and to teach.

The responsibility of the deacon is to assist the elders in spiritual and temporal matters. These responsibilities can be found in the books of Acts, Titus, and 1Timothy. Baptists adhere to the doctrine of the individual priesthood of the believer. Since Jesus Christ is our only intercessor, priests are not necessary. The function of a Baptist Pastor is substantially different than that of a Catholic Priest. The Priest (at least in theory) doles out salvation through the mass. He has authority through an "unbroken apostolic" line going back to Peter. His authority lies in the validity of proper ordination, with eighteen hundred years of tradition (which is viewed as equal in importance with scripture) at his disposal. The local congregation ordains a Baptist Pastor, with authority granted by scripture. He is to shepherd, preach, and teach, but salvation comes from Jesus alone. Baptists believe that every man and women will answer for himself or herself. Pastors will be judged on whether they correctly teach the word.

Historically, Baptists churches in America are traced to Roger Williams, in the colony of Rhode Island. Cairns says the following about the first Baptist church in America:

> The beginning of the Baptist churches in America was also associated with the swarming of the Puritans. Roger Williams (ca. 1603-83), who was educated for the Anglican ministry at Cambridge, soon adopted Separatist views. His independence of mind brought him to Boston from unfriendly England in 1631. He went from there to Plymouth because he thought the Boston Church had not purified itself sufficiently. For two years he ministered at Plymouth. When the church in Salem called him as Pastor in 1635, the General Court, inspired by

> John Cotton, interfered. It ordered him out of the territory under its jurisdiction within six weeks because he upheld the Indian ownership of land, opposed a state church, and insisted that the magistrates had no power over a mans religion. Leaving his wife and children in a mortgaged home, he plunged into the forest in the depth of winter and wandered until some friendly Indians gave him aid. In 1636 he purchased some land from the Indians and founded Providence. In 1639, a church was founded in Providence, and all members were rebaptized, including Williams. [52]

The Baptist message traveled forth from Rhode Island to Sandy Creek, North Carolina, then to South Carolina, and then throughout the colonies. Rhode Island College, which later became Brown University, was founded in 1764, to train ministers.

Presbyterian

The Presbyterian Churches grew from the work of John Calvin, and spread from Geneva to other parts of the continent, and then to Scotland. But not the works of Calvin alone assisted the meteoric growth in Scotland. It has been said that [53]Lutheran ideas laid the groundwork for the Reformation in Scotland under John Knox. Cairns describes the growth and development of the Scottish Church as follows:

> The Scottish church faced the problem of how to maintain the Presbyterian system of polity and the Calvinistic theology that it had adopted. For more than a century the Scots opposed the attempts to force the Episcopal system of

---

[52] Cairns, Earle E. 362-363

government on them. Not until James II fled from England and William and Mary took the English throne in 1690 was the Presbyterian church securely established as the national Church of Scotland.

From 1690 until 1847 the Scottish church was plagued with divisions over the question of lay patronage. Lay patronage meant that the crown or landlords could dictate the choice of a minister for a congregation. Many divisions occurred as the Scots fought for the freedom of their church. Ebenezer Erskine (1680-1754) was Deposed by the General Assembly of the Church of Scotland because he upheld the right of a congregation to choose its own minister. In 1733 he and others founded the Associate Presbytery which in 1740 became the Secession Church. This church split again in 1747 into two groups, but by 1820 most of the two groups merged as the United Secession Church.

Lay patronage also resulted in the founding of the Relief Church by Thomas Gillespie (1708-74) in 1761. The Relief Church and the United Secession Church united to form the United Presbyterian Church in 1847.

A more important schism occurred when Thomas Chalmers (1780-1847) led a group in the founding of the Free Church in 1843 over lay patronage AND the growing spirit of revival stimulated by the evangelical revival in Scotland. The Free Church became an aggressive evangelistic and missionary body. By 1868 it had eight hundred churches and nearly one thousand clerics. It united with the United Presbyterian Church in 1900 to form the United Free Church. The United Free Church combined with the Church of Scotland in 1929 to form the

> Kirk of Scotland because the right of lay patronage, the main cause of the division, had long since disappeared with the abolition of patronage by act of Parliament in 1874. Today the Church of Scotland is the major church in Scotland. [54]

This church is congregational in mode, but councilor in practice. The Presbyterian Church believes that the Church has replaced Israel as Gods chosen ones, and places the foundation of the church with the Abrahamic covenant. That being said, they are highly legalistic. The doctrine of this denomination is centered primarily on the [55]Westminster Confession, which sets forth the beliefs of the Presbyterian and Reformed Churches, and elaborates on the five points of Calvinism. These are as follows:

> Total Depravity – As a result of Adams fall, the entire human race is affected; all humanity is dead in trespasses and sin. Man is unable to save himself.
>
> Unconditional Election – Because man is dead in sin, he is unable to initiate response to God; therefore, in eternity past God elected certain people to salvation. Election and predestination are unconditional; they are not based on man's response.

---

[54] Cairns, Earle E. 413

[55] Boettner, Loraine. *The reformed Doctrine of Predestination.* 1

> Limited Atonement – Because God determined that certain ones should be saved as a result of Gods unconditional election, He determined that Christ should die for the elect. All of whom God has elected and Christ died for will be saved.
>
> Irresistible Grace – Those whom God elected and Christ died for, God draws to Himself through irresistible grace. God makes man willing to come to Him. When God calls, man responds.
>
> Perseverance of the Saints – The precise ones God has elected and drawn to Himself through the Holy Spirit will persevere in faith. None whom God has elected will be lost; they are eternally secure. [56]

Cairns has the following to say about the Presbyterian Church in North America:

> Many of the Scotch-Irish migrated to the colonies after 1710 because of economic discrimination practiced against Ireland by the trade laws of England. By 1750 about two hundred thousand had come to America. Many went to central and western Pennsylvania and became influential in the Pittsburgh area, which became a leading center of American Presbyterianism. By 1706 a presbytery had been organized in Philadelphia.[57]

---

[56] Enns, Paul. *Moody Handbook of Theology*, page 480
[57] Cairns, Earle E. 364

This church was introduced to North America by the Scottish immigrants, and has continued to grow ever since. This is the state church of Scotland.

Lutheran

The Lutheran churches grew out of Martin Luther's efforts at reforming the Roman Catholic Church. That being said, virtually all of the various denominations were a direct result of Luther's efforts. In the beginning, it must have appeared that there need be no splintering. Read what Cairns says of the early years of reform:

> Luther was indeed a national hero and held in high regard by prince, peasant, humanist, and knight alike; but his policies in the subsequent years alienated some of those who had followed him so readily at first. [58]

In fact, many complained that Lutheranism was to close to Roman Catholicism. As previously explained, the Lutherans believe in the doctrine of Consubstantiation, which is dangerously close to Transubstantiation. However, Luther replaced the idea of tradition and scripture with the idea of scripture alone as being authoritative. Lutheranism continued to grow in northern Germany, Denmark, Norway, Iceland, Sweden, and Finland. Lutheranism was introduced to North America By German and Scandinavian immigrants.

Episcopal

Today's Episcopalian church was yesterdays Anglican churches in America. The Anglican Church was introduced to North America by the Puritans, and eventually became the State Churches of the majority of the colonies. Cairns has this

---

[58] Cairns, Earle E. 285

to say in regards to the founding of the Anglican Church in the United States:

> The Virginia Company, which was given a charter in 1606 to settle and to exploit land in America, sent out settlers to Jamestown in 1607. Provision was made for the establishment of the Anglican Church. The colony did not prosper economically until 1619, at which point increasing numbers of Puritan Anglicans migrated to the colony. In 1624 the company was dissolved, and Virginia became a royal colony ruled for the King by a Governor. The Anglican church remained as the established church of the new colony. The Anglican church also finally became the established church of Maryland in 1702, despite Roman Catholic opposition. It was made the established church in parts of New York in 1693. An act of 1715 made the Anglican church the established church in North Carolina, and earlier, in 1705, it was established in South Carolina. Georgia accepted Anglican establishment in 1758.[59]

The Episcopalian churches are extremely liturgical, and the clergy are known as priests rather than Pastors. The church recognizes Sacraments in a fashion similar to the Roman Catholic Church, the main difference being that the clergy are permitted to marry.

Clericis Laicos (1298)

It is said that in times past laymen practiced great violence against the clergy, and our experience clearly shows that they are doing so at present, since they are not content to keep

---
[59] Cairns, Earle E. 358

within the limits prescribed for them, but strive to do that which is prohibited and illegal. And they pay no attention to the fact that they are forbidden to exercise authority over the clergy and ecclesiastical persons and their possessions. But they are laying heavy burdens on bishops, churches, and clergy, both regular and secular, by taxing them, levying contributions on them, and exhorting the half, or the tenth, or the twentieth, or some other part of their income and possessions. They are striving in many ways to reduce the clergy to servitude and to subject them to their own sway. And we grieve to say it, but some bishops and clergy, fearing where they should not, and seeking a temporary peace, and fearing more to offend man then God, submit, improvidently rather than rashly, to these abuses [and pay the sums demanded], without receiving the papal permission. Wishing to prevent these evils...and by our apostolic authority, we decree that if any bishops or clergy, regular or secular, of any grade, condition, or rank, shall pay, or promise, or consent to pay laymen any contributions, or taxes, or the tenth, or the twentieth, or the hundredth, or any other part of their income or of their possessions, or of their value, real or estimated, under the name of aid, or loan, or subvention, or subsidy, or gift, or under any other name or pretext, without the permission of the pope, they shall, by the very act, incur the sentence of excommunication. And we also decree that emperors, kings, princes, dukes, counts, barons, [etc.]...who shall impose, demand, or receive such taxes, or shall seize...the property of churches or of the taxes, or shall seize...the property of churches or of the clergy...shall...incur the sentence of excommunication. We also put under the interdict all communities which shall be culpable in such matters. And under the threat of deposition we strictly command all bishops and clergy, in accordance with their oath of obedience, not to submit to such taxes without the express permission of the pope...From this sentence of excommunication and interdict no one can be absolved except in the moment of death, without the authority and special permission of the pope...[60]

Unam Sanctam (1302)

The true faith compels us to believe that there is one holy catholic apostolic church, and this we firmly believe and painfully confess. And outside of her there is no salvation or remission of sins...In this church there is "one Lord, one faith, one baptism" [Eph. 4:5]...Therefore there is one body and of the one and only church, and one head, not two heads, as if the church were a monster. And this head is Christ and his Vicar, Peter and his successor...If therefore Greeks or anyone else say that they are not subject to Peter and his successors, they thereby necessarily confess that they are not of the sheep of Christ. For the Lord says in the Gospel of John, that there is one fold and only one shepherd [John 10:16]. By the words of the Gospel we are taught that the two swords, namely, the spiritual authority and the temporal are in the power of the church...Both Swords...the spiritual and the temporal, are in the power of the church. The former is to be used by the church, the latter for the church; the one by the hand of the priest, the other by the hand of kings and knights, but at the command and permission of the priest. Moreover, it is necessary for one sword to be under the other, and the temporal authority to be subjected to the spiritual; for the apostle says. "For there is no power but of God: and the powers that are ordained of God" [Rom. 13:1]; but they would not be ordained [i.e., arranged or set in order unless one were subjected to the other, and, as it were, the lower made the higher by the other...And we must necessarily admit that the spiritual power surpasses any earthly power in dignity and honor, because spiritual things surpass temporal things. We clearly see that this is true from the paying of tithes, from the benediction, from the sanctification, from the receiving of the power, and from the

---

[60] This edited version of the Papal Bull *Clericis Laicos* is taken from Perry M. Rogers *Aspects of Western civilization Volume I*, pages 367-368.

governing of these things. For the truth itself declares that the spiritual power must establish the temporal power and pass judgment on it if it is not good. Thus the prophecy of Jeremiah concerning the church and the ecclesiastical power is fulfilled: "See, I have this day set thee over the nations and over the kingdoms, to root out, and to pull down, and to destroy, and to throw down, to build, and to plant" [Jer. 1:10]. Therefore if the temporal power errs, it will be judged by the spiritual power, and if the lower spiritual power errs, it will be judged by its superior. But if the highest spiritual power errs, it can not be judged by men, but by God alone. For the apostle says: "But he that is spiritual judgeth all things, yet he himself is judged of no man" [1 Cor. 2:15]. Now this authority, although it is given to man and exercised through man, is not human, but divine. For it was given by the word of the Lord to Peter, and the rock was made firm to him and his successors, in Christ himself, whom he had confessed. For the Lord said to Peter: "Whatsoever thou shalt bind on earth shall be bound in heaven: and whatsoever thou shalt loose on earth shall be loosed in heaven" [Matt.16:19]. Therefore, whosoever resisteth this power thus ordained of God, resisteth the ordained of God, resisteth the ordinance of God [Rom. 13:2]...We therefore declare, say, and affirm that submission on the part of every man to the bishop of Rome is altogether necessary for his salvation. [61]

---

[61] This edited version of the Papal Bull *Unam Sanctum* is taken from Perry Rogers *Aspects of Western civilization Vol. I*, pages 369-368

Appendix B2
The Church and the Crusades; and The Knights of the Temple

The peasants Crusade: 1095-1096
The First Crusade: 1096-1099
The Second Crusade: 1147-1149
The Third Crusade: 1189-1192
The Fourth Crusade: 1202-1204
The Children's Crusade: 1202-1202
The Fifth Crusade: 1218-1221
The Sixth Crusade: 1228-1229
The Seventh Crusade: 1248-1254

Table 6. The Crusades.

Background

The crusades are an extremely misunderstood period of history. That is to say, they are misunderstood by both secular and Church historians. Secularists point to the crusades in an attempt to label all of Christianity as violent, evil, and bigoted. "More people have been killed in the name of Christ than any other" is a complaint that is often voiced. But this is unfair to both Jesus Christ and His church. While it is true that these events were violent, evil, and bigoted, it is equally true that these events do not represent the Church today. In fact, before we can even begin to understand the crusades themselves, we have to first understand the situation from the point of view of the churches, and in context of both the time period, as well as the culture of the day. And when I say churches, I mean both the Eastern Orthodox Church and the Roman Catholic Church. The very word *Catholic* is Latin for "universal", but differences in doctrine, as well as distance, had caused serious rifts within the church. There had been problems between Rome and Constantinople ever since Constantine the Great moved the capital of the empire east. The master of the Roman church wanted to be acknowledged as the Supreme ruler of the Church, and the Byzantine church wanted, well, just to left alone, actually. There were philosophical differences between the styles of worship between the east and the west, and the Byzantine church wanted to be left to worship in their own way. That is not to say that the Eastern church was less arrogant than Rome. Both churches claimed to be Caesar's inheritor, and both claimed exclusivity.

But the Patriarch of Constantinople did not desire to be acknowledged by all other Bishoprics as the one and only, master of all and everything spiritual beneath the heavens. Or rather, if he did, he knew was practical enough to know that it wasn't going to happen! The real down fall of Byzantium was the voracious spread of Islam.

Prior to the seventh century, the Roman church had enough to do just trying to tread water against the flood of invaders. But with the Turks "knocking at the door", and his former mercenary allies, the Norman's turned against him , Alexius, emperor of Byzantium, had nowhere left to turn except to the Pope. Now, it may seem as if this would be the last thing that the Byzantine emperor would do. And, if the Pope had been anyone but Urban II, the Byzantine emperor would certainly not have appealed to him for help. But Urban had learned from the mistakes of his predecessors. For instance, Alexius and all of his empire had been excommunicated by Pope Gregory VII. In 1089, Urban lifted the excommunication. Since the eastern church did not acknowledge the supremacy of the Pope, this act might seem to be an empty gesture, but in fact, it gave Alexius hope. Urban was waiting for an opportunity, and he wasn't to wait in vain. In 1095, Alexius sent a letter to Pope Urban requesting assistance, in the name of their common Lord. The letter contained reports of the abuses that were being perpetrated by the Turks. Young boys being circumcised, and positioned over the baptismal fonts so that their blood would pollute the water, women being raped, captured Christians of both the nobility and the peasantry being sodomized: what follows is an excerpt from the letter:

> "and, O misery, something that has never been seen before, on Bishops."[62]

Now this letter could not help but get the attention of the Pope. In fact, the situation seemed to be to good to be true. A plan began to germinate in the mind of the overjoyed Pope. He saw a Holy war, in which the west would rescue the east, and in so doing recover the lands which had been taken by the rampaging Moslems. And then, and even greater plan began to be formulated. The political situation in Europe was unstable, because only the eldest son could inherit. So this left the second, third fourth etc. etc. sons of the nobility land less and

---

[62] Robinson, John. *Dungeon, Fire and Sword*, Page 8.

destitute, and they were turning to banditry on an ever increasing basis.

And so, the plea of Alexius was, well, at least to Urban, a God-send. In one fell swoop, he would relieve the political situation (by giving the land less knights who joined the "holy war" the land that they recovered), he would strengthen the position of the church (because someone would have to coordinate the international efforts, and it certainly would not be the individual kings themselves!), and force the Eastern church to acknowledge him, the Pope, as the supreme ruler of the church! Certainly that would not be too much to ask for the rescuer of Byzantium?

And this is the situation that led to the crusades. Well, at least, this is a VERY simplified explanation, but it should do for our purposes, at any rate. And so began a pattern that would hold sway over the next few centuries. Land would be taken, and lost. The infidels would be driven back, and they would resurge.

The peasant's crusade and the first Crusade

As a result of Alexius' letter, Pope Urban II called the Council of Clermont. On November 27, 1095, Pope Urban called for a crusade against the "Saracens". The problem that was before the Pope was that, first of all, there were no such peoples as the Saracens! This term came to mean all the follower's of the Prophet of Islam. But in reality, when Alexius wrote his letter of 1095, he referred to the atrocities of the Turks on the Syrian border of his empire. The Greeks called these tribes *Sarakenos*. This specifically meant those Turks on the border. But this Greek phrase became "Latinized"
as the *Saracenus*, which in turn became , you guessed it, the Saracens.

Another problem that Urban had was that the so-called Saracens of Palestine were not evil, invading monsters, but rather, fairly tolerant Moslems who didn't mind at all the Christians or Jews who lived among them. But that didn't stop Urban. He worked himself, and consequently, the crowd gathered, into a frenzy of Hatred. As he wound up his diatribe, cry's of "Dues lo volt" (God wills it) began to peal through the square. This cry would eventually become the battle-cry of the crusaders. The crowd was overwhelmingly enthusiastic, and the Bishop of le Puy (It boggles the mind to consider that if the pope had hailed from this district, he would be known as "Papa le Puy") was the first to reach the Pope and beg permission to accompany the "holy army" on its quest to regain the holy land.

And so it began. Knowing that excessive time would cool the zeal of the nobility, Urban wasted none. The Bishop of le Puy, Adhemar, was to lead the Crusade, which was to leave by Autumn of 1096. Alexius had asked for a little help, but he was about to attempt to drink from a fire hose. Urban II was French by nationality, and so were most of the volunteers. But virtually all the nations of Christendom were represented.
(Incidentally, because most of the crusaders were French, the *Saracens* decided that they were ALL French, and consequently assigned the handle "Franj" to any crusader, no matter what his point of origin. It would seem that turn about is fair play.)

While Adhemar was Urban's choice to lead the crusade, another man decided that he had been divinely appointed as leader. He is remembered in the annuls of history as Peter of Amiens, or as Peter the Hermit. Now peter was definitely not what Urban had in mind when his fevered mind had envisioned the holy war, but Peter was among the first to decide to go. He began to preach up and down the land that it had been he who had convinced Urban to call for the crusade at the field of Clermont. Perhaps he even believed this to be true.

In point of fact, Peter had never been near the Pope. But he began to gather followers. Fifteen thousand of them, to be specific. Most of them were as ragged as he was, but several were of higher rank. One of these men, Walter Sansavoir was a French knight who brought a small army with him. (In spite of the meaning of his name, which translates as Walter the Penniless.) Peter's "crusaders" did not want to wait while the larger army was gathered, and so moved ahead. Because they did not have funds with which to secure supplies, they scrounged and pillaged toward Constantinople.

Alexius attempted to place supplies along the way, but they were inadequate, and so Peter's mob was half starved upon arrival. The Peasant army swelled to 20,000 along the way. Additionally, Peters ragtag mob had persecuted the Jews in every town on the way to Constantinople. Once their, the "army" behaved no better, and insisted to be transported
into Saracen territory. Although they had been instructed to await the arrival of the rest of the crusader force, Alexius was only too pleased to ferry them into enemy territory.

Once there, the lack of discipline and military experience made them easy targets. Although some of them would survive and join the larger crusader force, the majority of them were either killed or sold into slavery. Meanwhile, the real crusader force was arriving. Their behavior along the way was even worse than Peter's. At least to the Jews, who were wiped out as a warm-up for the upcoming main event. Having learned the hard way of western behavior from his experience with Peter the hermit, Alexius ensured that the Crusader forces were adequately fed. Additionally, the easterners constantly reminded the crusaders of the fabled wealth that lay on the other side of Constantinople. This was a vain attempt to get the Crusaders to hurry, and to leave Constantinople intact. Eventually they were ferried across to enemy territory, where they fought their first major battle for the city of Nicea.

After a hard fight, the crusaders had wrestled the enemy forces to the brink of surrender, and retired for the night, sure that the morning would give them victory. But alas, the city surrendered to Alexius in the night, leaving the "rescuers" with a goose egg. Apparently, the Saracens decided that the devil you know is better than the devil you don't know, and the crusading army woke to the sight of the standard of Byzantium flying over the city.

This annoyed the crusaders, but Alexius plied them with gifts, and, more importantly, with supplies. Since they liked to eat, they grudgingly gave in to the crafty Byzantine emperor. Alexius made the crusader's swear fealty to him personally, or threatened to take his ball and go home. Additionally, Alexius wanted Antioch returned to him. It stood in the crusader's path, and would have to be dealt with. Again, the crusaders had no choice but to agree. Alexius believed that the oath sworn by the crusader's would be binding. He was right, but only on his side. The crusaders would not keep their oaths, but would expect him to keep his.

Meanwhile, on to Antioch. October 21, 1097. Our hero's arrive before the city. Apparently they had been unaware of the size of the city, and of its awesome defenses. Siege warfare is difficult at best, but ridiculous when the city is a mile wide and three miles long! And such was the situation at hand. The crusaders sat.

And sat.

And sat.

And sat.

They sat through November. They sat through December. What a great way to celebrate Christmas! But at least they had entertainment. The ruler of the city had the Patriarch of

Antioch hung in a cage and dangled over the walls to discourage the invaders. They sat through January. They sat through February. In point of fact, they sat before the walls of Antioch from October 1097 until June 1098! And even when they achieved their goal, it wasn't through force of arms, but rather treachery. If Doctor Seuss had described this siege, it might have sounded something like this:

> *The knights and their people sat through the months, living in boredom and terrible funk. They waited and waited and waited some more, but try as they might, couldn't get through the door.*
>
> *They waited so long, in a terrible plight, but didn't give Antioch the least little fright! And then the commander got an idea so bright, an idea so evil, an idea not trite! It was a terrible, horrible, bloody idea! If through the front door by force could not go, perhaps then a traitor would help to do so!*
>
> *So they looked hard to find one. They searched high and searched low, and as usually happens, found someone willing to go!*

One of the Islamic Officers betrayed the city and opened a tower. What followed was a bloodbath. Every Turk in the city was butchered, man, women and child. No mercy was shown. This would set the tone for the campaigns to follow.

After the city was taken, Prince Bohemond of Taranto assumed control. Bohemond was the son of the Norman king Robert Guiscard. Bohemond did this in spite of the promise to return the city to Alexius. Apparently, a bird in the hand is worth two in the bush! So Antioch is in the hands of the Crusaders. And so was Edessa. Another of their number, a certain Baldwin, secured for himself the County of Edessa through deceit and treachery.

Now that they had taken Antioch, Jerusalem was with a ten day march. But at this point, Adhemar, Bishop of le Puy, contracted Typhoid and died. And, just as Urban had foreseen, without Papal control, the crusaders could not agree on anything. And so, they were stuck for almost a year in Antioch. It would be June of 1099 before they were at the gates of Jerusalem, and August before the city had fallen to them. The fight for the city was extremely brutal, and the butchered this time included the Jews of the city. [63]When the slaughter was complete, the priest Raymond of Aguilers quoted Psalm 118;

> "This is the day that the Lord has made, let us be glad and rejoice in it."

With the capture of Jerusalem, the crusaders control three of the four provinces that will make up the kingdom of Jerusalem. Before the crusaders took the city, they had been aided by the prior of a small order of monks who had run a hostel, or hospital, for pilgrims. As a result of the siege of the city, the monks had been expelled. This group was richly rewarded by the victors, and it was decided that the order should be expanded, and their duties expanded as well. They would now provide protection to the faithful.

And they became known as the Hospitallers of Saint John, or, as the Hospitallers.

The Knight's Templar

And so the crusaders had established, or were about to establish, a kingdom in the Holy Land. As a result of services rendered, Baldwin I, newly appointed king of Jerusalem, gave to the monks who had assisted him, gifts of money and grants

---

[63] Robinson, Jon. Page 118.

of land. Overcome by their good fortune, the master of their order decided two things.

First, that their role must be expanded from assisting pilgrims to protecting pilgrims. And in view of their expanded role, their patron saint, John the compassionate, would no longer suffice. And so, John the Baptist received the nod, and became the new orders patron. They became known as the Hospital of St. John of Jerusalem.

The expansion of the Knights Hospitallers had an immediate effect on a man named Hugh De Payens. Hugh was a vassal of the Count of Champagne, and he decided that, if it worked for the Hospitallers, it would work for him. So he asked the king of Jerusalem, Baldwin II, for permission to start a new order. While the Knights Hospitallers would continue to run hostels and hospitals, this new group would dedicate itself exclusively to guarding the shrines and holy places of the holy land.

This might seem like a strange concept to you and I, but you have to understand just what was going on economically at the time. The collapse of the Roman empire threw the world into a vacuum. Several replacements surfaced, but none lasted longer than the founder. History proves that, when there is an exceptionally able and competent king, usually an exceptionally incompetent and unable descendant will follow.

So the system we know as feudalism developed to fill the void. Feudalism has a strict hierarchy, with the upper nobility at the top, and the peasant at the bottom. It is a pyramid structure, with a broad base and a narrow peak.

When the Normans conquered most of Europe, the situation became even more bleak. Their system of inheritance allowed for only one inheritor. That is, only the eldest son could inherit. Most of these petty kings had several sons, and since only the eldest could follow, what could sons two through six do? Well, as members of the nobility, they were taught martial skills. Imagine the situation. Sons two through six, trained in individual combat, with no way to earn a living, and nothing to occupy his time. Additionally, combat equipment was extremely expensive. Remember, a knight needed armor, weapons, several horses, and a patron. This was long before the time of mass production, and a coat of chain mail cost an exorbitant sum. So did sword, shield, lance, mace and dagger. The chain mail not only cost a small fortune, it took time to manufacture, one ring at a time, and it took maintenance that was both expensive and time consuming. And horses. Each night needed at least two. One for war, and a lighter breed for travel. Every movie concerning chivalry ever filmed shows a brightly clad knight charging over the fields on a fast war horse. This is an incorrect image. A fully clad knight weighed more than a race horse could carry. Special breeds of horses were developed from stout farm stock. But these horses were to slow for regular travel. Yet more expense. So these excess sons traveled round fighting his fathers petty wars against neighboring petty nobility.

This was fine, until his father desired to make peace with his neighbors. Then the excess sons would loot and pillage wherever they could. This was bad for diplomacy, bad for chivalry, and bad for the church. Some of the excess sons could be trained for the church, but most were either unsuited or uninterested in clerical careers. And this is the political situation that Urban II's papacy presided over. So the idea of a crusade was a godsend. Sons two through six could now be sent safely into Saracen territory where they could fight to their hearts content. And when the Holy Land was captured, land would be available for everyone interested! But what to do when the crusade ends?

The first crusade was more successful than anyone dreamed possible. A new kingdom was carved. When the fighting was over, however, so was the unity maintained by the crusaders, and the army defending the newly formed kingdom evaporated, returning to their homes in the west. So when Hugh De Payens suggested a newly formed order of fighting monks, Baldwin II was willing to lend his support to the idea.

In the beginning, there were nine members of the newly formed order. Hugh De Payens was elected grand Master, and for the next nine years, the group was little more than a club. No members were recruited, and the order seemed destined to fade away. Then, in the year 1127, Baldwin decided that it was time for the order to expand. He wrote to Bernard of Clairvaux requesting that Bernard extend some of his political influence on the Pope to get him to officially sanction the new order. Why would Bernard be interested in an obscure order of men who wanted to fight the infidel. No one is really sure. Part of the reason may have been that Bernard saw himself as a potential member.

He was born of the knightly class, but was frail and sickly. Perhaps he wanted to fight the infidel vicariously. Perhaps it was the fact that his Uncle, Andre De Montbard (who would go on to become the fifth Grand master of the order, was a member. Whatever the reason, Bernard was interested. See appendix J for his response. Not only did he wield considerable influence on the pope, (Bernard was sometimes referred to as the "second" pope) but he personally wrote the charter and rules for the order. He based them loosely on the rules for the Cistercian order.

Organization

The Knights Templar were to be set up as follows:

There would be three separate branches of the order. The Knights themselves, the priests, and the Sergeants. The Knights had to be just that, knights. In order to apply for membership, one was required to be of the knightly class. That is, one had to be a member of the nobility. What would induce someone of this station to become a warrior monk? Because that is just what they would become. The vows of chastity and obedience were real vows, and when the pope sanctioned the new order, he made them responsible to him, and to him alone. So again, what would induce a member of the knightly class to become a warrior monk? I have already demonstrated the deplorable economic conditions in Europe during this time period. One thing the prospective knight could expect was arms and armor. And Horses. And an attendant to help him with those same arms and armor previously mentioned.

Another benefit was respect. The new knight would join an order formed and obedient directly to the pope. And purpose. He would fight the infidel in the holy land. It was a win-win situation. The Knights gained the advantages already mentioned, the pope gained an army answerable only to him, and Baldwin gained permanently garrisoned troops.

The second branch was the priests, and they functioned exactly as you might expect, except that they answered to no bishop. And the third branch was made of free born men-at-arms. So Bernard fully supported the order, and called for gifts from throughout Europe. The Count of Champagne gave generously, and not just because his cousin was among the founding members, but because he believed in the purpose. And so the order had funds, affiliation, and purpose. But what made theses men tick? In what ways were they normal monks? In what ways did they differ?

They had daily prayers, like monks of any other order, but they had to maintain fighting physiques and care for weapons and equipment. Since they required heavy exercise, it was necessary that they eat more meat than the usual monk. Immediate obedience to superiors was called for. In a world of rugged individualists, the Templars required discipline. And what better way to maintain this discipline than to establish a splendid esprit-de-corps?

Chastity was another important element. Knights were not permitted to even touch a member of the opposite sex. Not even their mothers or sisters. To ensure that this was rigidly adhered to, and to prevent homosexuality among themselves, the Templars wore a belt-like garment around their midsections. Templars were not permitted to bathe with any regularity, and, in an age when Europeans went clean-shaven, the knights wore full mustaches and beards. This made them stand out among their fellow Europeans, but it served a different purpose when they would fight in the Middle East. In stark contrast to the Europeans, the Moslem men wore beards. They did not respect the clean-shaven crusader, whom they regarded as effeminate. But they would build a healthy respect for the Knights Templar. And the Beards helped initially. The bravery in battle displayed by the Templars didn't hurt, either.

The Templars get rich

The Templars role in the various crusades is beyond the scope of this paper. Suffice it to say that they were active in the Holy Land, as well as in the European crusades. Some of the decisions of the Grand Masters were wise, some foolish. But the fame and fortune of the Templars grew. In fact, that was the element that eventually led to the demise of the order. As their fame grew, so did their pride. Because they answered only to the pope, they alienated may important clerical figures.

As there fame grew, so did donations. The order owned land throughout Europe. After the fall of Jerusalem, however, the order seemed to lose purpose. It is hard to be a Knight Templar when there is no temple. True, the order had gained some powerful allies (Richard the Lionhearted comes immediately to mind), and indeed, the order would continue to hold the favor of the English Kings right up to the end, but it had also gained powerful enemies.

The chief amongst these was the king of France. Philip IV, also called "the fair". Philip was a ruler with grandiose visions for France. And these plans required funds. Philip actually recalled all the coinage within his realm, had it melted down, and replaced the coins with more coins of lesser value. At one point, he enraged the people so much that he had to seek refuge in the Templar conclave in Paris. During his "visit" with the Templars, Philip became aware of just how wealthy the Templars actually were.

Since they answered only to the pope, the Templars were exempt from taxation. During the crusades, the Templars had invented a way to become even richer. They made it possible for a young man to travel from London to Jerusalem without having to carry chests of currency with him. In what may be the earliest case of actual international banking, the Templars made it possible to deposit funds in the Temple complex at, say, London, and be given in return a letter of credit, which would be honored at the headquarters in

Jerusalem. No fuss, no muss, just instant funds. Of course, this service didn't come free. Or even cheap. And so the Templars just got wealthier and wealthier. And Philip discovered this immense wealth.

But how to get it? Since the Knights were clergy, they were protected. And since they answered only to the pope, they were doubly protected. So Philip accused the knights of heresy, and pressured his pet pope, Clement V, to enforce his desire.

And so it came to pass, on Friday the thirteenth, October 1307, that the order went out to arrest every Templar in France. But some escaped, either through luck, or advance notice given by supporters. And Templars in other countries were not initially arrested. Spain, for instance, never did obey papal orders. They had enough problems trying to drive out the infidel. And Edward II in England had no interest in arresting and torturing his friends the Templars. In point of fact, when the pope ordered him to do so, he reluctantly had them arrested, but sent word to the holy father that he was unable to comply with the orders to torture, because Englishmen were unaccustomed to this practice, and he had no one with the necessary skill! But the pope sent him some torturers. Wasn't that thoughtful of the pope? At any rate, most of the Templars in England escaped to Scotland.

Robert the Bruce didn't care what your political leanings were, if you could swing a sword, you were welcome. (He was having problems of his own with Edward II).

And so died the order. Or did it? But that is another story entirely…

Appendix C
Exegetical Word Study: Babylon

Babylon

Βαβυλῶνι

Βαβυλών (12)

There are over 236 usage's of the word within the Septuagint.

Strong's

Βαβυλών   G897; Of Hebrew origin [H894]; *Babylon*, the capital of Chaldaea (literally or figuratively as a type of tyranny):—Babylon.

בָּבֶל H894; bâbel *baw-bel'*. From H1101; *confusion*; *Babel* (that is, Babylon), including Babylonia and the Babylonian empire:—Babel, Babylon.

בָּלַל H1101; bᵉlîyaʻal *bel-e-yah'-al*. A primitive root; to *overflow* (specifically with oil); by implication to *mix*; also (denominative from H1098) to *fodder:*—anoint, confound, X fade, mingle, mix (self), give provender, temper.

בְּלִיל H1098; bᵉlîyl *bel-eel'*. From H1101; *mixed*, that is, (specifically) *feed* (for cattle):—corn, fodder, provender.

Thayer's

Βαβυλών. Babylon = "confusion"

1) a very large and famous city, the residence of the Babylonian kings, situated on both banks of the Euphrates. Cyrus had formerly captured it, but Darius Hystaspis threw down its gates and walls, and Xerxes destroyed the temple of Belis. At length the city was reduced to almost solitude, the population having been drawn off by the neighboring Seleucia, built on the Tigris by Seleucus Nicanor.

2) of the territory of Babylonia

3) allegorically, of Rome as the most corrupt seat of idolatry and the enemy of Christianity

Citing in TDNT: 1:514, 89;

Total KJV Occurrences: 12
Matt 1:11-12 (2), Matt 1:17 (2), Acts 7:43, 1 Pet 5:13, Rev 14:8, Rev 16:19, Rev 17:5, Rev 18:2, Rev 18:10, Rev 18:21

Vincent's Word Studies

Babylon. Some understand in a figurative sense, as meaning "Rome"; others, literally, of "Babylon," on the Euphrates River. In favor of the former view are the drift of ancient opinion and the Roman Catholic interpreters, with Luther and several noted modern expositors, as Ewald and Hoffmann. This, too, is the view of Dr. Cook in the "Speaker's Commentary." In favor of the literal interpretation are the weighty names of Alford, Huther, Calvin, Neander, Weiss, and Reuss. Professor Salmond, in his admirable commentary on this epistle, has so forcibly summed up the testimony that we cannot do better than to give his comment entire: "In favor of this allegorical interpretation it is urged that there are other occurrences of "Babylon" in the New Testament as a mystical name for Rome (Rev 14:8; 18:2,10); that it is in the highest degree unlikely that Peter should have made the Assyrian Babylon his residence or missionary center, especially in view of a statement by Josephus indicating that the Emperor Claudius had expelled the Jews from that city and neighborhood; and that tradition connects Peter with Rome, but not with Babylon.

The fact, however, that the word is mystically used in a mystical book like the Apocalypse-a book, too, which is steeped in the spirit and terminology of the Old Testament-is no argument for the mystical use of the word in writings of a different type. The allegorical interpretation becomes still less likely when it is observed that other geographical designations in this epistle (1 Peter 1:1) have undoubtedly the literal meaning. The tradition itself, too, is uncertain. The statement in Josephus does not bear all that it is made to bear. There is no reason to suppose that, at the time when this epistle was written, the city of Rome was currently known among Christians as Babylon. On the contrary, wherever it is mentioned in the New Testament, with the single exception of the Apocalypse (and even there it is distinguished as 'Babylon, the great'), it gets its usual name, Rome. So far, too, from the Assyrian Babylon being practically in a deserted state at this date, there is very good ground for believing that the Jewish population (not to speak of the pagan) of the city and vicinity was very considerable. For these and other reasons a succession of distinguished interpreters and historians, from Erasmus and Calvin, on to Neander, Weiss, Reuss, Huther, etc., have rightly held by the literal sense."

Robertson's word Pictures

She that is in Babylon, elect together with you *hee* (NT:3588) *en* (NT:1722) *Babulooni* (NT:897) *suneklektee* (NT:4899). Either actual Babylon or, as most likely, mystical Babylon (Rome) as in the Apocalypse. If Peter is in Rome about 65 A.D., there is every reason why he should not make that fact plain to the world at large and least of all to Nero.

TDNT (Selected portions)

1. Apart from references to the Babylonian captivity in Matthew 1:11, 12 and 17 and Acts 7:43, and the single reference in 1 Peter 5:13, the term Βαβυλών is found only in the Apocalypse, where it is applied in a most significant manner for the ungodly power of the last time: Βαβυλὼν ἡ μεγάλη (14:8; 16:19; 17:5; 18:2; 10, 21). The great city (17:18; 18:10; 16, 18, 19, 21). The destruction of Babylon is proclaimed by an angelic voice in 14:8. The place of the fall of Babylon in the apocalyptic drama (with the outpouring of the

7th vial) is indicated in 16:19. Then in 17:1 to 19:10 the divine expressly portrays this city and its 7 visions. He paints it in the symbolical form of a harlot: the great whore (17:1; 19:2), the mother of harlots and the abomination of the earth (17:5). She sits on a beast with 7 heads and 10 horns, strikingly adorned. Her name is written on her forehead. She is drunk with the blood of the saints slain within the city (17:16). It is God who will thus bring judgement on the city (17:17; 18:8; 19:2). At its fall there is no jubilation in heaven but sorrow among the inhabitants of the earth (c. 18).

The most important features of this picture are taken from the OT prophets. This is true even in the name Babylon. The historic city and empire of Babylon were always depicted by the prophets as the ungodly power par excellence. Thus even after the fall of Babylon, Babel, as they saw it, represented for later Jewish readers of scripture, and also for early Christians, the very epitome and type of an ungodly and domineering city. The localisation of which might vary with the current historical situation. The image of the whore also comes from the OT. Tyre is thus named in Isaiah 23:15, and Nineveh in Nahum 3:4. In addition, the same picture is often used in connection with the idolatry of Israel. The image of the beast is taken even in detail from Daniel 7. Thus we might well say that the whole depiction of the Apocalypse, esp. c. 18, is made up of OT thoughts and expressions rather after the manner of a mosaic.

The sayings of Jesus have also had their influence on the shaping of the visions. Thus, for the heavenly command to depart from Babylon we have models in Isaiah 48:20; 52:11; Jeremiah 50:8; 51:6 etc. on the one hand, but also in Matthew 24:15 and par on the other. In revelation 18:21 we have a mixture of Jeremiah 51:63 and Matthew 18:6 and par. Perhaps we also see an influence of Matthew 23:25 (cf. 23:27) on Revelation 17:4 (the golden cup full of abomination and impurity).

Many other traditional features must have passed into the visions of the divine which we cannot now track down in detail. Thus the fact that the women sat on the beast (which is disregarded in the interpretation in 17:7 and even contradicted in 17:16), probably derives from the writers acquaintance with pictures of a goddess or god riding on a beast. Again she holds a cup in her hand, and the question arises whether this feature is suggested by depictions of goddesses with the horn of plenty.

All these different elements are arranged by the divine in his visions into a great and uniform whole in which he sees part of what is going to take place in the immediate future (Revelation 1:1). He knows that the city which is to be destroyed is already present, Revelation 17:18: ἡ γυνὴ . . . ἔστιν ἡ πόλις (article) ἡ μεγάλη ἡ ἔχουσα (present) βασιλείαν ἐπὶ τῶν βασιλέων τῆς γῆς. This can only Rome. The main arguments for this area. Revelation 17:9: the city lies on 7 hills; b. it was common for later Judaism to apply to Rome the title Babel as a type of ungodly power.

2. In 1 Peter 5:13 also, where we have greetings from the Christian church εν Βαβυλῶνι to the churches of Asia Minor, the reference can only be to Rome. The essential reasons for this, apart from those already mentioned, are a. the general application to Rome in early exegesis, with only a few trifling exceptions; the lack of even a hint that Peter ever stayed or worked in the land of Babylon, as distinct from the fairly solid historicity of his stay and martyrdom in Rome.

If we accept this reference to Rome in 1 Peter 5:13, then we must follow Schlatter in his deduction "not merely that Peter expects the destruction of Rome and sees it in the prophetic utterances against Babylon, but that the whole Church both in Rome and Asia Minor shared this view.

New Unger's Bible Dictionary

BAB'YLON (bab'i-lon). An ancient city-state in the plain of Shinar, derived from Hurrian papil.

Name. The name is derived by the Hebrews from the root balal ("to confound") and has reference to the confusion of tongues at the Tower (Gen 11:9). Thus the biblical writer refutes any God-honoring connotation of the name. The biblical account ascribes the founding of the ancient prehistoric city of Babylon to the descendants of Cush and the followers of Nimrod (10:8-10). This statement distinguishes the people who founded the city (evidently the Sumerians) from the Semitic-Babylonians who afterward possessed it.each side. It had two walls, inner and outer. The vast space within the walls was laid out in streets at right angles to each other, lined with houses three to four stories in height. He lists the following chief public buildings: the temple of Bel, consisting of a tower in the shape of a pyramid, more than eight stories, topped with a sanctuary; the palace of the king; the bridge across the Euphrates connecting the eastern and western sections of the city. Herodotus described the city as overwhelming in its size (1.178-86). The next Greek writers whose records are important are Ctesias and Diodorus Siculus (2.7-8). According to them the city was much smaller than Herodotus had represented, its circuit being 360 stades (41 miles, 6 yards). To the bridge of Herodotus, Diodorus has added a tunnel under the river and describes the hanging gardens of Nebuchadnezzar as rising in terraces, which supported full grown trees. Hebrew accounts represent the city as great in size, beauty, and strength; in this they were amply sustained by the inscriptions and excavations. As a matter of fact, excavations show that Babylon was smaller than ancient Greek writers said. The wall was about eleven miles long and eighty-five feet thick and was protected by a moat filled with water from the Euphrates. Actually the wall was double: the outer wall was twenty-five feet thick and the inner one twenty-three feet thick with an intervening space filled with rubble. Watchtowers stood sixty-five feet apart on the walls. Eight or nine gates pierced the wall. The population of greater Babylon (the walled city and its suburbs) in Nebuchadnezzar's day has been estimated at about a half million.

Beginnings. The beginnings of the city of Babylon are unknown to us except for the biblical passage mentioned earlier (Gen 10:10). About 1830 B.C. the city began its rise to prominence. In the ensuing struggle with surrounding city-states, Babylon conquered Larsa and the First Dynasty of Babylon was established. Such kings as Sumu-abu, Sumla-el, Sabum, Apel-Sin, and Sin-mu-ballit ruled. Then the great Hammurabi (which see), ascended the throne about 1728-1686, and conquered not only all of S Babylonia but extended his conquests as far N as Mari. At this famous city on the middle Euphrates, Andre Parrot, excavating for the Musee du Louvre (1933ff.), unearthed thousands of cuneiform tablets, a vast royal palace, a temple of Ishtar, and a ziggurat.

The city of Babylon did not reach the height of its glory, however, until the reign of Nebuchadnezzar II (605-562 B.C.). Nebuchadnezzar made the city splendid, and the king's own inscriptions are concerned largely with his vast building operations. Babylon was excavated thoroughly by the Deutsche Orientgesellschaft under the direction of Robert Koldewey, 1899 to 1917 (cf. Das wieder erstehende Babylon, 4th ed. [1925]). Nebuchadnezzar's brilliant city included vast fortifications, famous streets such as the Processional, canals, temples, and palaces. The Ishtar Gate led through the double wall of fortifications and was adorned with rows of bulls and dragons in colored enameled brick. Nebuchadnezzar's throne room was likewise adorned with enameled bricks. The tall ziggurat was rebuilt. This, Herodotus said, rose to a height of eight stages. Near at hand was Esagila ("whose housetop is lofty"), the temple of Marduk or Bel, which the king restored. Not far distant were the "hanging gardens," which to the Greeks were one of the seven wonders of the world. How well the words of Dan 4:30 fit this ambitious builder: "Is this not Babylon the great, which I myself have built as a royal residence by the might of my power and for the glory of my majesty?"

The splendid Babylonian Empire of Nebuchadnezzar was destined soon to fall. He was succeeded on the throne by Amel-

Marduk (561-560), the Evil-merodach of 2 Kings 25:27. This man was murdered by his brother-in-law, Nergal-shar-usur (559-556), whose son ruled only a few months and was succeeded by one of the conspirators, who did away with him. A noble named Nabunaid, or Nabonidus, then ruled, together with his son Belshazzar (555-539; see Dan 5); Nabonidus was the last king of the neo-Babylonian Empire. On October 12, 539 B.C., Babylon fell to Cyrus of Persia, and from that time on the decay of the city began. Xerxes plundered it. Alexander the Great thought to restore its great temple, in ruins in his day, but was deterred by the prohibitive cost. During the period of Alexander's successors the area decayed rapidly and soon became a desert. From the days of Seleucus Nicator (312-280 B.C.), who built the rival city of Seleucia on the Tigris, queenly Babylon never revived.

Size and Appearance. Herodotus says the city was in the form of a square, 120 stades (13 miles, 1,385 yards) on each side. It had two walls, inner and outer. The vast space within the walls was laid out in streets at right angles to each other, lined with houses three to four stories in height. He lists the following chief public buildings: the temple of Bel, consisting of a tower in the shape of a pyramid, more than eight stories, topped with a sanctuary; the palace of the king; the bridge across the Euphrates connecting the eastern and western sections of the city. Herodotus described the city as overwhelming in its size (1.178-86). The next Greek writers whose records are important are Ctesias and Diodorus Siculus (2.7-8). According to them the city was much smaller than Herodotus had represented, its circuit being 360 stades (41 miles, 6 yards). To the bridge of Herodotus, Diodorus has added a tunnel under the river and describes the hanging gardens of Nebuchadnezzar as rising in terraces, which supported full grown trees. Hebrew accounts represent the city as great in size, beauty, and strength; in this they were amply sustained by the inscriptions and excavations. As a matter of fact, excavations show that Babylon was smaller than ancient Greek writers said. The wall was about eleven miles long and eighty-five feet thick and was protected by a moat filled with water from the Euphrates. Actually the wall was double: the outer wall was twenty-five feet thick and the inner one twenty-three feet thick with an intervening space filled with rubble. Watchtowers stood sixty-five feet apart on the walls. Eight or nine gates pierced the wall. The population of greater Babylon (the walled city and its suburbs) in Nebuchadnezzar's day has been estimated at about a half million.

The Figurative Meaning. In the prophetical writings, when the actual city is not meant, the illustration is to the "confusion" into which the whole social order of the world has fallen under Gentile world domination (Luke 21:24; Rev 6:16). The divine order is given in Isa 11, that is, Israel in her own land the center of divine government of the world and the medium of the divine blessing, with Gentile nations blessed when associated with Israel. Anything else is politically mere "babel." In the NT Babylon prefigures apostate Christendom, that is, ecclesiastical Babylon, the great harlot (Rev 17:5-18). It also prefigures political Babylon (17:15-18), which destroys ecclesiastical Babylon. The power of political Babylon is destroyed by the glorious second advent of Christ (Rev 16:19; 18:2-21).

The Future Location of Babylon

Much has been written concerning the prophecy of Isaiah in regards to the location of future Babylon. Isaiah 13:20 says:

> [19]And Babylon, the beauty of kingdoms, the glory of the Chaldeans' pride, will be as when God overthrew Sodom and Gomorrah. [20] It will never be inhabited or lived in from generation to generation; Nor will the Arab pitch *his* tent there, Nor will shepherds make *their flocks* lie down there.

Many expositors believe that this is fulfilled prophecy. But it must be pointed out that Babylon has never been totally uninhabited. Much has been written claiming that the city was abandoned. This is simply not the case. Extrabiblical sources laim that an extremely large Jewish settlement lived six miles outside of Babylon. Another account had a synagogue located in Babylon proper, not more than a mile away from the fabled temple of Marduk. Nor is it abandoned today. Saddam Hussein began rebuilding the city, on its original location, in the mid 1980's. I believe that the destruction spoken of in Isaiah is as yet unfulfilled.

Βαβυλών 897. (12)

1. **Matt 1:11** - Josiah became the father of Jeconiah and his brothers, at the time of the deportation to Βαβυλῶνος.

This refers to the Babylonian exile, and as such refers to the city itself. In point of fact, all of the references in Matthew, as well as the single reference to the city in Acts, are in reference to the Mesopotamian city.

2. **Matt 1:12** - After the deportation to Βαβυλῶνος Jeconiah became the father of Shealtiel, and Shealtiel the father of Zerubbabel.

All of the Matthew and Acts uses are Genitive.

3. **Matt 1:17** (2) - o all the generations from Abraham to David are fourteen generations; from David to the deportation to Βαβυλῶνος, fourteen generations;
and from the deportation to Βαβυλῶνος to the Messiah, fourteen generations.

4. Acts 7:43 - 'You also took along the tabernacle of Moloch and the star of the god Rompha, the images which you made to worship. I also will remove you beyond Βαβυλῶνος.'

5. **1 Pet 5:13** - She who is in Βαβυλῶνι, chosen together with you, sends you greetings, and *so does* my son, Mark.

The only dative form in of the word found within the New Testament.

6. **Rev 14:8** - And another angel, a second one, followed, saying, "Fallen, fallen is Βαβυλὼν the great, she who has made all the nations drink of the wine of the passion of her immorality."

All of the usage's of the word in the book of Revelation are Nominative.

7. **Rev 16:19** - The great city was split into three parts, and the cities of the nations fell. Βαβυλὼν the great was remembered before God, to give her the cup of the wine of His fierce wrath.

8. **Rev 17:5** - and on her forehead a name *was* written, a mystery, "Βαβυλὼν THE GREAT, THE MOTHER OF HARLOTS AND OF THE ABOMINATIONS OF THE EARTH."

Ryrie's Notes: *BABYLON THE GREAT*. Though the famous city of Babylon was on the Euphrates River, the name here seems to be a symbolic reference to Rome (see v. 9 and 1 Peter 5:13). In chap. 17 Babylon represents the false religious system that will center in Rome during the Tribulation. In chap. 18 it represents more the political and commercial aspect of the revived Roman Empire headed by Antichrist. Thus the term stands both for a city and for a system (religious and commercial) related to the city (much like "Wall Street," which is both a place and system). For other references to Babylon, see Gen. 10:10; 11:9 ("Babel"); Isa. 13:19-20; Jer. 50-51. *MOTHER OF HARLOTS.* The family of false religions is unfaithful to the Lord and thus is described as a harlot (vv. 1, 15-16).

9. **Rev 18:2** - And he cried out with a mighty voice, saying, "Fallen, fallen is Βαβυλὼν the great! She has become a dwelling place of demons and a prison of every unclean spirit, and a prison of every unclean and hateful bird.

10. **Rev 18:10** - standing at a distance because of the fear of her torment, saying, 'Woe, woe, the great city, Βαβυλὼν, the strong city! For in one hour your judgment has come.'

11. **Rev 18:21** - Then a strong angel took up a stone like a great millstone and threw it into the sea, saying, "So will Βαβυλὼν, the great city, be thrown down with violence, and will not be found any longer.

Observations

1. This particular word can refer to either a city, an empire, or a symbolic world system.

2. Whenever there seems to be a symbolic reference, the word is always used with the description "great" or "the great;" as in "Babylon the Great," or the great city,".

3. In every case that the adjective is used, it is a form of the following: μεγάλη. Adjective Nominative Feminine Singular, of μέγας. Dictionary entry: μέγας, μεγάλη, μέγα. The meaning of the word: large, great (of a loud sound; strong wind; high fever; etc.); greatest; surprising (2 Cor 11:15).

6. Whenever the word is used without the adjective, it would appear to be a reference to an actual location, rather than symbolic.

Conclusion

Although some expositors have concluded that the reference in 1 Peter 5:13 is symbolic of Rome, the usage of the word in this case is similar to the usages in the books of Matthew and Acts, where the reference is clearly to the city of Babylon. As this writer has clearly demonstrated, the opinions as to the meaning of the term are diverse.

Kittel absolutely states that the location is a symbolic reference to Rome. Of course, this conclusion is partly based on the faulty idea that there is "the lack of even a hint that Peter ever stayed or worked in the land of Babylon, as distinct from the fairly solid historicity of his stay and martyrdom in Rome."

This writer would assert that the scripture itself is evidence, and would further assert that there is very little evidence aside from tradition that Peter ever visited, let alone was martyred, in the vicinity of Rome. The only other argument is an argument from silence, unless on accepts the verse in its literal sense. Because Peter used the word without the adjective, as well as Peter's straight forward personality, this writer must conclude that he is writing from the city of Babylon on the Euphrates river, where a large number of Jews were living, and had lived, since the exile. And the writer is not alone in this conclusion. Dr. J. Vernon Magee has this to say:

> I think "Babylon here means Babylon, although some think it is a figurative name for Rome. Simon Peter is to practical to have used a figurative term.

It is important to note that the actual location, whether in the city of Babylon or Rome, does not change the meaning of the passage. It is interesting to discuss, but the message that the apostle means to convey is the same regardless of where it was written from.

Note: This word study is in the format recommended by Dr. John Grassmick.

Appendix D
Selected Bibliography

Aland, Kurt. *The Greek New Testament with Dictionary.* Edmonds: United Bible Society 1966.

Anders, Max. *30 Days to Understanding the Bible.* Dallas: Word 1988.

Anders, Max. *The Holy Spirit in 12 Lessons.* Nashville, Tennessee: Thomas Nelson, 1995.

Barclay, William. *The LETTERS of John and Jude (Revised Edition).* Philadelphia: The Westminster Press, 1976.

Boettner, Loraine. *The Reformed Doctrine of Predestination.* Philadelphia, Pennsylvania; The Presbyterian and reformed Publishing Company, 1978.

Bruce, F. F. *The Canon of Scripture.* Downers Grove, Illinois.: InterVarsity Press, 1988.

Bruce, A. B. *The Training of the Twelve.* Grand Rapids: Kregel 1971.

Bullinger, Ethelbert William. *Figures of Speech Used in the Bible.* Grand Rapids: Baker Book House, 1968.

Cairns, Earle E. *Christianity Through the Centuries.* Grand Rapids, MI; Zondervan Publishing House, 1996.

Calvin, John. *Institutes of the Christian Religion.* Grand Rapids: WM. B. EERDMANS PUBLISHING COMPANY. 1970.

Chafer, Lewis Sperry, *He that is Spiritual.* Grand Rapids, Michigan: Zondervan Publishing House, 1967.

Chafer, Lewis Sperry, *Grace.* Grand Rapids, Michigan: Kregel Publications, 1995.

Chafer, Lewis S. *Systematic Theology (Volume One; Abridged Version).* USA: SP Publications. 1988.

Comfort, Wesley P., ED, *The origin of the Bible.* Wheaton, Tyndale House Publishing, 1992.

Criswell, Wallie Amos. *Why I Preach that the Bible Is Literally True.* Nashville: Broadman Press, 1969.

Custer, Stewart. *Does Inspiration Demand Inerrancy?* Nutley, N.J.: Craig Press, 1968.

Enns, Paul, *The Moody Handbook of Theology.* Chicago: Moody Press, 1989.

Evans, Tony. *Our God is Awesome*. Chicago, Moody Press: 1994.

Gangel, Kenneth O. *Feeding & Leading*. Grand Rapids: Baker 1989

Gaussen, L. *The Inspiration of the Holy Scriptures*. Chicago: Moody Press, 1949.

Geisler, Norman L. and Nix, William E. *A General Introduction to the Bible*, Chicago, Moody Press, 1968.

Geisler, Norman L, ed. *Biblical Errancy, An Analysis of its Philosophical Roots*. Grand Rapids: Zondervan Publishing House, 1981.

Geisler, Normal L., and William E. Nix, *From God to Us*, Chicago, Moody Press, 1974.

Geisler, Norman L. *Christian Apologetics*. Grand Rapids: Baker.

Gonzalez, Justo L. *The Story of Christianity, Volume I*. San Francisco: Harper Collins Publishers, 1984.

Gonzalez, Justo L. *The Story of Christianity, Volume II*. San Francisco: Harper Collins Publishers, 1985.

Grassmick, John D. *Principles and Practice of Greek Exegesis* Dallas: Dallas Theological Seminary 1974.

Gregg, Steve. Ed. Revelation -- Four Views, A Parallel Commentary. Nashville: Thomas Nelson Publishers, 1997.

Halley, Henry H. *Halley's Bible Handbook*. Grand Rapids: Zondervan, 1927.

Henry, Matthew. *Matthew Henry's Commentary on the Whole Bible.* USA: Hendrickson Publishers, Inc. Eighth printing- December, 1997.

Hodges, C. Zane. *The Greek New Testament according to the Majority Text.* Nashville: Nelson, 1985.

House, H. Wayne - Ed. *Chronological and Background Charts of the New Testament.* Grand Rapids: Zondervan, 1981

Ice, Thomas. *Fast Facts on Bible Prophecy.* Eugene, Oregon: Harvest House Publishers. 2001.

Jensen, Irving L. *Jensen's Survey of the New Testament.* Chicago: Moody, 1981.

Jensen, Irving L. *Jensen's Survey of the Old Testament.* Chicago: Moody, 1978.

Jeremiah, David. *The Handwriting on the Wall.* Dallas: Word, 1992.

Kahler, Clay A. *Simple Theology; Theology for the rest of us.* Eugene, Oregon: Wipf and Stock Publishers, 2002.

Kent, Homer A. *Jerusalem to Rome Studies in Acts.* Grand Rapids: Baker, 1972.

Kent, Homer A. *The Epistle to the Hebrews.* Winona Lake: BMH Books, 1972.

Kent, Homer A. *The Pastoral Epistles (1 & 2 Timothy and Titus). Winona Lake:* BMH Books, 1986.

Kubo, Sakae. *A Reader's Greek-English Lexicon of the New Testament.* Zondervan, 1972.

LaHaye, Tim F. *Revelation – Illustrated and Made Plain*. San Diego: Family Life Seminars Publications, 1973.

LaHaye, Tim F. Charting the End Times. Eugene, Oregon: Harvest House Publishers, 2001.

Laird, Harris R., *Inspiration and Canonicity of the Bible*. Grand Rapids: Zondervan Publishing House, 1957.

McGee, J. Vernon, *Thru the Bible Vol. 4*. Nashville, Tennessee: Thomas Nelson Inc., 1983.

Nave, Orville J. *Nave's Topical Bible*. Peabody: Hendrickson Publishers.

Pentecost, J. Dwight. *Things To Come - A Study in Biblical Eschatology*. Grand Rapids, Michigan: Zondervan Publishing House, 1958.

Perschbacher, Wesley J. *The New Analytical Greek Lexicon*. Peabody: Hendrickson, 1990.

Rogers, Perry M. *Aspects of Western Civilization, Volume I*. Englewood Cliffs, New Jersey; Prentice Hall, 1992.

Rogers, Perry M. *Aspects of Western Civilization, Volume II*. Englewood Cliffs, New Jersey: Prentice Hall, 1992.

Ryrie, Charles C. *Basic Theology*. Chicago: Moody Press, 1999.

Ryrie, Charles C. *Balancing the Christian Life*. Chicago: Moody Press, 1994.

Ryrie, Charles. Ed. *New American Standard Ryrie Study Bible (Expanded Edition)*. Chicago: Moody Press, 1995 Update.

Ryrie, Charles Caldwell. *Dispensationalism Today*. Chicago: Moody Press, 1965.

Ryrie, Charles C. *Balancing the Christian Life*. Chicago: Moody, 1969.

Ryrie, Charles C. *So Great Salvation*. Chicago: Moody, 1997.

Ryrie, Charles C. *The Holy Spirit*. Chicago: Moody, 1965.

Saucy, Robert L. *The Church in God's Program. Chicago:* Moody, 1972.

Sauer, Erich Ernst. *From Eternity to Eternity*. Grand Rapids: Wm. B. Eerdmans Publishing Co., 1954.

Shinn, Garland H.., *The Doctrine of the Bible*. Notebook published by the author.

Strong, James. *The New Strong's Exhaustive Concordance of the Bible*. Nashville: Nelson, 1964.

Sullivan, James L. *Baptist Polity – As I See It*. Nashville, TN; Broadman Press, 1983.

Summers, Ray. *Essentials of New Testament Greek*. Nashville: Broadman & Holman, 1995.

Thomas, Robert L, Ed. *Exhaustive Concordance of the Bible* (NAS). Anaheim: Foundation Publications, Inc., 1998.

Turabian, Hate L., *A Manual for Writers of Term Papers, Theses, and Dissertations Fifth edition*, Chicago, University of Chicago Press, 1987.

Unger, Merrill F. *The New Unger's Bible Dictionary*. Chicago: The Moody Bible Institute. Revised and Updated Edition, 1988.

Unger, Merrill Frederick. *Principles of Expository Preaching*. Grand Rapids: Zondervan Publishing House, 1955.

Vedder, Henry C. *A Short History of the Baptists*. Valley Forge: Judson Press, 1907.

Vine, W. E. *Vine's Complete Expository Dictionary*. Nashville: Nelson, 1984.

Vine, W. E. *Vine's Complete Expository Dictionary of Old & New Testament Words*. Nashville: Nelson, 1984.

Wallace, Daniel B. *Greek Grammar Beyond the Basics*. Grand Rapids: Zondervan 1996.

Wallace, Daniel B. *The Basics of New Testament Syntax*. Grand Rapids: Zondervan, 2000.

Walvoord, John F. and Roy B. Zuck. *The Bible Knowledge Commentary (New Testament)*. Colorado Springs: Victor, 1983.

Walvoord, John F., *The Holy Spirit*. Grand Rapids, Michigan: Zondervan Publishing House, 1991.

Walvoord, John F. and Roy B. Zuck. *The Bible Knowledge Commentary (Old Testament)*. Colorado Springs: Victor, 1983.

Walvoord, John F. *Jesus Christ Our Lord*. Chicago: Moody, 1969.

Walvoord, John F. *The Holy Spirit.* Grand Rapids: Zondervan, 1954.

Wilkinson, Bruce and Kenneth Boa. *Talk thru the Bible.* Nashville: Nelson, 1983.

Wood, Leon J. *A Survey of Israel's History.* Grand Rapids: Zondervan, 1970.

Wood, Leon J. *The Prophets of Israel.* Grand Rapids: Baker, 1972.

Zuck, Roy B. *Basic Bible Interpretation.* Colorado Springs: Chariot Victor Publishing. 1991.

Zuck, Roy B. - Ed. *A Biblical Theology of the New Testament.* Chicago: Moody, 1994.

www.ingramcontent.com/pod-product-compliance
Lightning Source LLC
Chambersburg PA
CBHW051737230426
43670CB00012B/2057